Spirit Keeping: A Guide for Spirit Keepers

by Magnolia & Ash West

© 2010 by the author of this book (Magnolia & Ash West of Creepy Hollows).
The book author retains sole copyright to his or her contributions to this book.

Table of Contents

Introduction..06
Question & Answer Section..08
    Spirit Keepers..08
    Spirit Origins...09
    Spirit Binding & Spirit Keeping........................11
    Spirit Interaction...25
    Spirit Care..29
    Spirit Limitations...32
Bringing Spirits Home...36
How Many Spirits Should I Keep?.............................39
What Should I Look For?...41
Getting Entities for a Specific Purpose......................43
Getting Started...47
    Associations & Offerings................................51
    Connecting With Spirits..................................54
    Invocations for Connection.............................55
    Meditating With Spirits....................................59
    Altars/Sanctuaries...60
    Tips, Tricks, & Tidbits......................................61
Will Spirit Keeping Work for Me?...............................63
Help! I Can't Feel My Spirit!......................................65
How-To Protect Your Spirited Vessels.......................71
The Well-Rounded Collection....................................73
The Dark Truth...78
How? Binding, Vessel Selection, & Spirits................81
Limitations, Powers, & Manifestations......................85
Misconceptions: Anything Goes in the Spirit World...87
Myths, Lies, and Other Fabrications of Knowledge...91
The Different Realms..99
What is Spiritualism?...101
Spiritualism vs. Religion..104
Conclusion..107
Dictionary of Common Terms..................................110
Pages for Your Notes...114

Spirit Keeping: A Guide for Spirit Keepers

This book is dedicated to all the members of the Creepy Hollows site who have given so much to each other & to the community as a whole every day, to all the practitioners who were along our side in paving the way for Spirit Keeping to be public on the internet, and to all those who will become Spirit Keepers in the future. Let your adventure begin…

Introduction

Who are we & why are we writing this book? We are among the few who brought Spirit Keeping to the public eye. Our site is currently the largest, most traversed web site dedicated to Spirit Keeping & all things paranormal. Since we've already virtually written the book on Spirit Keeping we're putting it down on paper.

We here at Creepy Hollows follow a path of the paranormal that has lain obscure for hundreds of years. The traditions passed through families, alliances, & groups of common interest are those we have brought to light in the past years building one of the fastest growing paranormal communities existing online. We are Spirit Keepers.

Spirit Keeping provides the means of direct spirit interaction & communication through the use of conjuration practice. This means you read an invocation or perform a ritual based on the type of entity in order to bring forward a spirit of that race who wishes to communicate with you. They include spirits of beings that lived on Earth, in other realms (astral or spiritual), and/or other dimensions. It also includes conjuring immortals of various origins.

Once a spirit or immortal has been conjured you can choose to create a temporary line of communication & interaction or a permanent connection. A temporary connection would fall into the category of "unbound" spirits; spirits who have no further direct tie to you. A permanent connection is known as a "bound" spirit. This means you are creating a permanent binding to a vessel (a tangible item or your spirit) that is a direct line of communication & interaction to you. It does not mean the spirit is actually bound to a vessel & no longer able to roam freely.

A bound spirit means the spirit has an access point for communication & interaction that leads directly to you, which makes you a "Keeper". You can call upon them when you need to, and they have the freedom to be with you or be in their own realm.

Spirit Keeping enriches the lives of those who participate in a vast number of ways. Not only does it provide a unique & special insight into a particular race of being, it can also provide insight into specific times in history, ancient civilizations, other realm civilizations, powers & abilities humans do not possess, and a valuable wealth of knowledge that cannot be otherwise obtained.

So many have asked us if we had a book, we decided that it would be a good idea to have a physical copy in-hand rather than just a large site to sift through. Sometimes it's nice to curl up with a book rather than be tied to a computer chair. When we decided to take this task on we asked the members of our site to tell us what questions they had when they were first starting out, or what questions they still had. These questions comprise our Q&A sections, and we hope that it helps those who are new to the Spirit Keeping community. You may find redundancy in some sections of the book. This is not unintentional; sometimes when learning something new to hear the same thing applied in different ways helps to understand the whole scope of what you are trying to understand.

Q&A: Spirit Keepers

Who are Spirit Keepers? Thousands across the globe of varied backgrounds, religions, lifestyles, genders & ages. They are those who carry the belief of the paranormal & metaphysical in their hearts every day; finding the beauty that exists beyond the power of the human eyes.

They work with spirits through various venues of communication including meditation, telepathy, pendulum, automatic writing, and dreams. They welcome spirits into their lives and make them part of their family.

Why are you Spirit Keeping? There may be multiple answers to this question and that is perfectly normal. Spirit Keepers do so for companionship, to learn about different worlds & periods of time, to strengthen natural abilities, to develop extra abilities, to learn about spell casting, the paranormal & magic and a host of other reasons... the primary of which is just naturally being drawn to them.

Some work with spirits to enhance gifts such as psychic power, clairsentience, and other forms of mancy. Others work with spirits to learn about different periods of time and other realms in their pursuit of discovery. Some work with spirits in complement to their spell casting & magic because spirits can offer insight, assistance & support through energy & power; most do so to share life & company.

The practice of this branch of the paranormal is based strongly on Spiritualism and being spiritual should be not confused with being religious. Those who practice Spiritualism come from many & varied backgrounds of religious subscription, or lack thereof.

Q&A: Spirit Origins

Where do spirits come from? Simply explained, the physical, spiritual & astral planes. They come from any entity that has lived & died on any of the planes and those who are immortal on any of the planes.

Why do they want to be kept? Spirits want the ability to communicate, share, and be part of something. Spirits do that by coming into our lives themselves or by being invoked or conjured. Once they have come to us they can stay of their own will, attach themselves to a person or vessel, or be bound temporarily or permanently to a person or vessel. No one wants to think that after they have gone there will be no purpose or usefulness to their lives.

Many have reported being "haunted" by loved ones or ancestors, these reports coming even from those who are not typical subscribers to the paranormal. This is no different in the aspect of spirits from our own realm & other realms; they too wish to be of purpose & assistance. Some are set on accomplishing help with a particular human whereas others roam unbound until there is a specific need for their guidance, support, help, friendship, companionship, etc.

They have the capability of being on our realm as well as the spiritual realm, and in the case of those who originated from the astral realm or spiritual realm some have the capability of walking all 3 planes. This accounts for why sometimes their presence is more strongly felt than others. They aren't always sitting around waiting for something to happen; they are capable of coming & going to and from you to their own realm on their own.

Why would they need a home? They don't need a home, many spirits desire a home. They enjoy being a part of something

Spirit Keeping: Q & A

much like we as humans enjoy being part of the lives of other humans, animals & nature. Spirit Keeping is not a new tradition; variations of Spirit Keeping have been performed in civilizations around the world for thousands of years.

Why are there so many spirits? Simply explained, they are from the physical, spiritual & astral planes. They come from any entity that has lived & died on any of the planes and those who are immortal on any of the planes. The world we know of has existed for billions of years and in those billions of years billions of entities have lived & died right on this planet.

When any living being dies it moves into spirit form. The worlds outside of our own Earth & solar system have existed for billions of years and on their own planes & dimensions have had their own beings that have lived & died as well as Immortals who have no expiry on life. They come to us as unbound spirits, through conjuration for binding, through summoning for temporary contact, through visions & extra sensory means of contact, and through various forms of invocation for temporary or long-term contact. This includes spirits & entities from our own realm as well as those who exist in all the dimensions & galaxies on the physical, spiritual, and astral planes... resulting in an infinite number of entities & spirits available for contact & interaction. There is no lack of beings & entities who have lived between the 3 realms and all the dimensions & galaxies existing within those realms.

Q&A: Spirit Binding & Spirit Keeping

What is binding? It is a permanent act performed with a spirit or a spell. In the case of a spirit it is a mutual agreement transacted between a conjurer/practitioner & a spirit for the spirit to be associated with an object or person. When a spirit or enchantment is bound to someone or something that binding act is a permanent placeholder for the spirit or spell. When a spirit is bound to a person or bound to an object that is a permanent act that creates a haven for the spirit. The vessel, be it person or object, is the physical realm binding site which remains unless purposefully dissolved by the person.

How do you bind? There can be multiple ways to go about this; a practitioner can do it as part of the conjuration, you can use pre-cast tools like Binding Bags, Boxes, or amulets, or use a specially written spell or ritual to do so.

Is Spirit Keeping dangerous? In a nutshell, no. It is imperative that you work with a trusted practitioner who knows what they are doing and has a good reputation for providing bindings of exactly what is promised. Aside from that, and if you are working with a trusted practitioner, if you exercise respect & caution there is nothing to fear. Those who live in the paranormal know Hollywood & TV programs dramatize the spirit world for sensationalism.

There are different methods of classification for spirit such as White Arts & Dark Arts. White Arts being entities solely of positive light & do no harm. Dark Arts being entities, like human beings, who can make the decision to be bad or good; and vary from average to very bad. Black Arts are only recommended for extremely experienced people as their intent is solely bad and nothing good can come of an inexperienced Keeper having a BA entity in their home. As long as you assess who you are, for what reason you are becoming a Spirit Keeper, and what aspects of yourself or your life you want to complement or enhance you will be well-informed.

There are outlets for support to provide guidance & answer questions such as our forum. You can always garner support & assistance from others who are Spirit Keepers. It is important to know from who you are gaining your wisdom & guidance as some are not truly knowledgeable and may steer you in the wrong direction. With the Dark Arts & especially the Black Arts never bring anything into your home that you are not prepared to care for & treat with the proper respect. Spirit Keeping is not dangerous with White Arts entities & spirits at all, and hardly an issue with Dark Arts when you are well-informed.

What are White Arts, Dark Arts, & Black Arts? White Arts means the spell or spirit is purely good in its intentions; it is not capable of being bad. It is a positive, uplifting, and heart-warming energy. Dark Arts simply means it's like a human being; capable of being good or bad. In the case of spirits they likely choose to do the right thing, as most humans do, but they have the freedom of choice. Black Arts means the entire intent of the spell or spirit is to be malicious & perform functions of harm to others.

What is involved in keeping a Dark Arts spirit? They can bring a different type of adjustment; sometimes causing nightmares, bad luck, overwhelming physical reactions such as headaches or joint aches. For most these subside in the first week, sometimes up to two weeks. They aren't evil or out to cause problems. As previously explained being classified as Dark Arts means it can choose right or wrong.

With that in mind there are times when a DA spirit may be obstinate, a prankster, bring on dark energies & feelings, but for the most part you'll find it no different than being around any human companion

How do you know that the right spirit came through & not a bad spirit? If you have an experienced conjurer/practitioner, then you know the difference in energies from long-term exposure & experience. I would know a Vampire from an Angel in a split-second during the conjuration process because their energies

Spirit Keeping: Q & A

are very different.

The odds you use a Djinn invocation & a Fae comes through is next to nothing. Invocations, when properly written, conjure only the intended target & nothing else. This is why it's important to work with an experienced & respected practitioner.

Otherwise, you leave yourself open to chance. With venues like eBay you don't know who the people are or how experienced or intelligent they are in the practice of spirit conjuration. They could be fresh out of the gate, in which case they shouldn't be working with anything too complicated, and if they did it could cause some real issues. Most people on eBay don't state where they learned how to do what they do, and what their ideology or methodology is.

Do I need to do any invocations or rituals to get them to work with me? Some practitioners may have their own way of going about things but the majority of spirits do not require any kind of simple or elaborate invocation or rituals. Portal keys & invocations may be used to help encourage communication & manifestation in some cases but it is not required as a part of interacting & being a companion to a spirit. Some spirits may require an invocation, but the number is few. We will review ways of communicating with your spirits in a separate section.

How do you conjure? Depending on the entity this occurs through a method of words spoken and/or written, certain actions or movements being performed, and most importantly the education & training in conjuration that allows you to perform a conjuration effectively.

As there are thousands of entities to consider not all methodologies can be reviewed, however, there are often multiple ways to conjure one type of spirit or one race of spirit. You can conjure a specific entity within a race or you can conjure an entire race. For example, you can conjure the goddess Aphrodite, you can conjure the primordial, Grecian gods, or you can conjure the entire Grecian god hierarchy.

Spirit Keeping: Q & A

Another example, you can conjure a Marid Djinn, or all Arabian Djinn, or all ancient, Arabian Djinn, etc. Depending on the conjuration & actions involved depends on the broad or specific terms through which you are working with a spirit or race of spirits.

What is a custom conjuration? It's when a practitioner conjures a race of entity or spirit with the intention of finding a spirit or entity that specifically wants to be with the person they are conjuring for.

How do you know a spirit wants to be with someone? For a practitioner this occurs when you feel or hear the spirit calling to the person. In a custom conjuration only those who wish to be companion to the person respond.

For the Keeper they will know because the spirit bonds with them. It is important to work with a practitioner or seller you trust & you know has a good reputation in the field of Spirit Conjuration & Spirit Keeping because often it is the discretion of the practitioner to make the decision of which spirit goes with which person.

An experienced practitioner will make the best decision as their experience will be important in discerning the correct spirit for each Keeper. As a Keeper when it comes to your decision in choosing a pre-bound spirit you should take into consideration the immediate reaction & gut instincts in reading or seeing the spirit. There is no substitute for the immediate, positive kinship you feel towards a spirit

Is keeping spirit slavery? You may think that keeping the Fae, Djinn, Unicorn, and other Creatures is a form of slavery as they are bound permanently to a vessel...that's not quite the case. When an entity dies their spirit is released and becomes unattached. It is free to exist and roam without restriction anywhere. Most of the time the spirits disappear never to be heard from again and perhaps once in awhile a human may encounter a temperature change, energy disturbance or

Spirit Keeping: Q & A

see/feel/hear something they can't explain and it might be the spirit of one of these entities.

However, when they are bound to a vessel it gives them a home, a sanctuary, the ability to belong and participate in an active lifestyle and you will find that they become "alive" again. They want to feel loved, wanted, and fulfilled the same as when they existed in their original form. It is not like trapping a genie inside of a bottle as folklore reads, the spirit isn't actually trapped inside of the vessel like a prison, the vessel is an attachment to them so they have immediate access to you and vice versa. Also, having a vessel allows you to cast additional amenities such as protection spells, enhancing spells, and other enchantments that provide them assistance in the physical realm. No spirit is bound against their will.

You will find that giving an entity a home that doesn't have one makes them grateful and they want to do anything to please because it lets them know they are not forgotten and you have the great privilege of being part of an entity that hasn't existed on the earth's soil for sometimes thousands of years. It is a preservation of their culture, race and beliefs and that makes them immortal and that makes them happy. That is why we go through such pains to bind the spirits of any and all entities we can find to give them a home, make them feel loved and not let those who lived here even before humans become forgotten.

If you have spirits does it attract more spirits? No. The only spirits who will come to you are those looking to share time with you. Unbound spirits are not uncommon and their presence amongst humans is a regular occurrence whether the person believes in spirits or not. They move & exist just as we do and coming into contact with an unbound is a certainty for every human being on Earth. Welcoming spirits into your home doesn't make you any more or less susceptible to other spirits.

Is Spirit Keeping evil? Absolutely not. Spirit Keeping is a voluntary process on both ends; they volunteer to be with you and you volunteer

Spirit Keeping: Q & A

to have them with you. It is absolutely not a religious action as anyone of any belief system can welcome spirits into their lives and at our site there are people from all religious subscriptions who are Spirit Keepers. It is a non-discriminatory lifestyle anyone can be a part of.

What is Bridging? It is a process invented by Creepy Hollows where the spirit or spell is bound to both a vessel & the Keeper. This gives the Keeper the freedom of having the spirit with them without having to have the vessel. It allows them to call the spirit to them when they desire as well as sending the spirit back to the vessel if needed. In the case of spells it allows the Keeper the ability to call upon the power of the spell whether they have the vessel with them or not.

What kind of manifestations can I expect? Manifestations can vary depending on the spirit or entity but you can typically expect to see orbs, light streaks, Shades, mist, blurry apparitions, audible sounds, words, or noises, and to have manifestations of true form in dreams or visions. Some races of entities share common manifestations, however, it is up to each individual spirit to decide how they are going to manifest to their Keeper. Most spirits choose a method of manifestation that is most comfortable & most recognizable to their Keeper so it results in a greater bond & greater chance of interaction. Manifestations can be abrupt or slow to form. They can be long-term or temporary. Each spirit & relationship has to be taken on its own merit.

How quickly do spirits contact you? For some this happens before the spirit even arrives at their home. For others the contact can be anywhere between a few days to a few months. It truly depends on the type of spirit or entity and how social an entity they are.

Sometimes spirits will not contact you until they are needed, whereas others are more companion-like and are friendly & active. Your effort & energy put into the relationship is what you will derive. It is not advisable for you to rely on others to be a go-between for you & your spirit(s). Channelers, psychics, and

Spirit Keeping: Q & A

readers are valuable assets to the paranormal community for many reasons; however they should never be a substitute for you creating interaction & contact between you & your spirit(s).

If you do not take responsibility to strengthen & grow your paranormal energy for contact & interaction with spirits you will never obtain the ability to know what is truly going on with your spirits and you will be vulnerable to rely solely on the words of others. If you are going to embark on the adventure of Spirit Keeping you should be ready, willing, and able to put forth the effort of bonding & initiating contact with spirits or you should not be a Spirit Keeper.

What happens if I ignore my spirits because I'm sad, busy, etc? The spirits with you are very much aware of your life & what is going on with you. The majority of the time they know you better than you know yourself and they are not going to be upset if you have to take time away from them to address your own issues. They are highly evolved beings who see the bigger picture and they chose you knowing all that would transpire, so don't worry if you have to take time away.

What should I do when I bring a spirit home? First, and foremost, spend time with them. Include them in your life, talk to them, and share the things that happen with them... treat them as you would any friend. It is a simple act to bond and you don't have to do anything outlandish or change your entire life to enjoy the company of a spirit. You should always consult with your practitioner or seller to see if the method they bound the spirit with requires any additional steps, invocations, etc.

Speaking solely for Creepy Hollows bound spirits & bindings you do not have to do anything special or perform any specific ritual, invocation, etc in order to welcome a spirit into your home.

You can use the associations provided for entities through the Creepy Hollows Encyclopedia if you wish, and you can make offerings to the spirits in your home in order to show your

Spirit Keeping: Q & A

appreciation for them, but nothing will replace or be more effective than time spent with your spirit & involving them in your life.

How do you bond with a spirit? Include them in your life; talk to them, share things with them, treat them as a friend. You can make offerings to them, do things for them you know they would like, and the best place to derive that information is in the Creepy Hollows Encyclopedia which lists associations & tips on bonding with entities.

Can someone else touch my spirit's vessel? As water & salt touching your vessel doesn't hurt the binding or spirit, it should not make a bit of difference whether someone else touches your spirit's vessel or not. Any practitioner worth their weight in gold will bind the spirit so it is protected & shielded and someone else touching it isn't going to matter at all. You can even take an extra step to add something like the Creepy Hollows Dead Spell which renders a vessel "dead" or "empty" when touched and no one is the wiser of the vessel's true purpose.

However, you should always consult with your practitioner or seller to ensure a binding has been performed that cannot be manipulated by someone else touching the vessel. It is often thought that someone touching your vessel will cause the spirit to be confused and not be able to differentiate between your energy & the other person's energy. This is not an accurate portrait of the relationship between Keeper & spirit. A spirit responds to a specific person because they appreciate your energy. Spirits are not dim-witted entities that are easily confused & manipulated just by someone else's energy being introduced into the equation. They have been differentiating between energies long before you existed.

How is a spirit bound to my spirit? Binding a spirit to your spirit should never be mistaken for soul binding. Your spirit & your soul are two very different things. Binding to spirit means binding to your essence, the field of energy that comprises your

Spirit Keeping: Q & A

unique spirit, which some believe is split into pieces & reincarnated, while your soul moves on to whatever you believe is your version of Heaven.

If someone tells you Binding to Spirit means soul binding you can tell them they are ignorant of the facts. Having a spirit bound to your spirit is typically not noticeable in any way to you in terms of feeling like there is something extra inside you or experiencing anything out of the ordinary with your physical body. Most don't even experience anything they would not experience by having a vessel instead.

Is direct-binding better than having a vessel? For the purpose of interacting & bonding with a spirit it does not make a difference. For each Keeper, though, this will be a personal preference. Some report having a spirit bound to their spirit results in faster bonding times and better interaction, others report the same results in having the spirit bound to a vessel. This is something that each Keeper will discern not only for themselves but likely also on a case-by-case basis. In my opinion Bridging is the ultimate option because it allows you to have the spirit with you or with its vessel allowing you the freedom of options.

Can spirits make you twitch, move, or be paralyzed? No, but energy can and when you are introducing another energy-driven entity into your home there can be a period of adjustment because of the increase of energy. Typically most Keepers don't see any difference at all with the influx of energy, but some have reported temporary side effects. It is always prudent to err on the side of safety if you are experiencing any twitching, shaking, moving, or any other physical action to make sure it isn't medical.

How can I tell what class level my spirit is, even if it's not from CH? If you want to use the Creepy Hollows Class Rating scale to classify your spirits it is best to obtain a set of our calibrating stones so you can compare the energy of the stone to the spirit in your keep.

Spirit Keeping: Q & A

What determines the class rating? For Creepy Hollows work we determine the Class Rating based upon the strength & energy of the spirit and/or spell involved.

How can I tell that this spirit is here, and is actually in the vessel? As with any industry there are going to be people who are fake. This is unavoidable and the best way to keep yourself from being taken is to stick with practitioners who have earned good reputations amongst collectors. Unfortunately, because of unscrupulous sellers writing bad things about the competition all over the internet the best way to truly get an accurate portrait of a practitioner is to contact their clients. With eBay, you can see their clients in their feedback, and with websites if they have a forum you can join and see what the response & atmosphere is like on their site. To see if a spirit is truly with you, the best way is to trust your gut instinct & your natural senses to see if you detect an additional presence with you. It can be difficult to put the trust solely in yourself, but by doing so you are gaining the strength & ground to build your own abilities & sensitivities.

Don't dismiss even the smallest of paranormal occurrence as sometimes spirits introduce themselves gradually rather than being immediately in your face.

What happens if I want to keep a spirit that when alive liked tropical weather but I live in the snowy mountains? When an entity was alive it had a climate to which it was best suited. Some, like humans, could adjust to a varying degree one way or another, but even those who had a strict climate requirement, now that they are in spirit form, are no longer tied down by those restrictions. While they may appreciate their climate when alive it is not necessary to keep a Mermaid in water, a Barbegazi in snow, or a Brass Dragon in the desert now that they've moved to spirit form.

Can I loan my spirit to someone or give my spirit a task to do for someone else? Some spirits, like Volkhs or Wraiths, are very good at

Spirit Keeping: Q & A

being tasked for yourself or someone else. In general most spirits won't mind if you request they help a loved one or friend because they care about you & want to help you in any way. Be sure you ask the spirit before you offer their assistance to someone else.

Is there anything that I can do that will accidentally release my spirit? No. Any practitioner worth their weight in gold will bind properly so the spirit cannot be released by accident.

Can someone with more experience steal my spirits away from me? No. Why? To unbind you must know the process in which it was bound, you cannot transmute any bound spirit without their permission, and you cannot forcibly bind spirits whose vessels are lost without their permission.

Not only that, but conjurer/practitioners have no reason to try; they are capable of conjuring spirits so why would they want to do that when they can conjure what they want?

Binding isn't a simple thing you can do without either training or without a tool already prepared with the necessary enchantments for you to activate. Unbinding requires you to know how it was bound in order to deconstruct the binding and reverse the process. Not to mention, any worthy conjurer/practitioner will place certain enchantments on their bindings to safeguard the spirits & spells from anyone trying to be bothersome.

Is collecting only for people that were born with psychic ability already developed? No, you do not need to have psychic abilities in order to be a paranormal collector. Everyone has a gift of sensitivity when they are born however slight or greatly it has naturally developed. Anyone can work on their sensitivity and grow their ability to sense the paranormal energies around them.

Spirit Keeping: Q & A

What do I do when I feel like the energy of a vessel is too strong for me and makes me dizzy, gives me headaches, etc? Acclimating to a new spirit or new binding can take up to a week for some. If it is causing problems or interruptions to your daily life you should move the vessel to a non-community area of your home where you least frequent. This way the energy still has a chance to work with you, but it's not in a place you are occupying frequently and you're not feeling the full effect of the binding.

Why are some vessels more expensive than others, when the material may not even be real gemstones? Practitioners typically price bindings by the complexity of the work performed, and then add in the cost of the vessel. When purchasing in the paranormal community you have to remember you're buying what has been done to the vessel, not the vessel alone.

How do I keep my spirits or spelled vessels from being detected by other people that don't share my beliefs? Most of the time, no one will know. If someone is sensitive they may suspect there is something or sense an unfamiliar energy from the vessel, but they aren't going to know exactly what is different. Most spirits won't make themselves known to outsiders or without their Keeper's permission. If you choose, there are spells which render a vessel completely "empty" to any outsider who comes into contact; sensitive to energy or not (ours is called the "Dead Spell").

What is the difference between binding & attachment? A binding is the permanent & direct binding of a spirit, energy, or spell to a location (vessel, person, etc). An attachment is temporary; usually done by energies or spirits themselves. They attach themselves to a location (vessel, person, place, home, etc) and they can stay as little or as long as they wish. Either the spirit or energy can remove themselves and/or the person who owns the location can remove them.

Spirit Keeping: Q & A

When conjuring to sell, what makes a spirit not be a suitable choice for binding, whether the spirit is white, grey, or darker? A practitioner who is experienced & is well-trained will know when a spirit is unsuitable for binding. Spirits who are bound should be willing, possess the desire to interact with humans, and express a desire to conduct themselves within the boundaries of mortal life. This means not coming forward to incite, antagonize, or otherwise inflict undesirable energy to the mortals they come in contact with.

It is no different than who you choose to be with in life; you wouldn't choose to be friends with someone you know isn't good for you & a practitioner should never choose a spirit they know isn't good for being bound. This is a reason you should always work with an experienced & respected practitioner

Are all spirits bound with cloaking? Cloaking is the methodology of providing the spirit & vessel the ability to be undetectable by any outsider without the express permission of the spirit. An inexperienced practitioner may not know enough to provide this, but it should be a staple in any binding. Spirits do not want public display & unwanted attention any more than you would enjoy living in a home with a constantly open front door & open windows.

Where do spirits get their names? Is it their real name or is it an English version of it? In some cases it is their name when living, in other cases it may be the human version of their name or a name they have adopted once in spirit form. The origin of the names of spirits is varied, and depends on the type of spirit. In some cases the origin of the spirit may be a language or communication system completely inaccessible to humans, therefore providing it would be impossible for us to understand. For reasons such as this some choose to adopt a name.

Is body material needed for any part of spirit binding? No. It should not be necessary to provide any hair, skin, fingernails, blood, or any other bodily issue in order to perform a binding.

Spirit Keeping: Q & A

Strongly question any practitioner who asks you for it.

Is a birth date needed? Depending on the type of binding & its complexities you may be asked, but you do not see this often in Spirit Conjuring & Binding, because experienced practitioners normally do not need it. This is more commonly needed in some magic & spellwork.

Can you summon a Dark Arts creature with a White Arts conjuration and make them White Arts? No, you cannot make a DA entity WA, or vice versa. That would be like trying to make a giraffe human, if it isn't that way you aren't going to make it that way by just changing the words you conjure it with. You cannot use a DA conjuration with WA, or vice versa.

Can anyone learn to conjure and bind spirits? Yes. They have to really have the passion, respect, and humility to become a successful conjurer/practitioner. Anyone can learn if it is truly something they want.

Where can I learn to do this? You can learn by taking classes from an already established practitioner, or by being taken on as an apprentice to an established practitioner.

Q&A: Spirit Interaction & Communication

My spirit says "such and such" according to the pendulum, and I think it's not getting along with me or another spirit, but can I trust the answers? Your intuition is the most important thing you will develop as a Spirit Keeper. If you feel uneasy about an answer you are receiving then you should take heed of that gut instinct and find an alternate way to investigate the situation. You can use tools like a pendulum, tarot cards, automatic writing, scrying balls, etc. or go with your intuitive thought & gut instinct. The longer you are a Keeper the more exact your energies are going to become in discerning communication from spirits.

How do I know if my spirit wants to be with a new keeper? The majority of the time spirits do not want to be re-homed because they chose to be with you in the first place. However, there are times when spirits are with you only for a season; for a purpose of fulfilling something to assist you. If you feel that a spirit truly does want to be re-homed you should find an outlet where you can find the next person right for them. An example of this would be the CH Marketplace or eBay. However, make sure that they truly want to be re-homed and it isn't you projecting your doubts or insecurities.

How do I find out the name, age, and looks of my spirits? Most practitioners will enclose a brief description of the spirit if it is applicable to the type of entity. If they do not and you want to see what your spirit looked like when they were alive the best thing to do is to ask the spirit to manifest to you in a thought, dream, or vision. If you prefer to work with tools, you can use your pendulum or cards for answers. However, we strongly recommend you ask the spirit to manifest to you.

Spirit Keeping: Q & A

How do I find out what types of activities my spirits will enjoy? That is definitely going to be part of your adventure! Learning about your spirits & learning what things in your life they connect with & enjoy is part of the adventure of the journey. You can also use the associations of each entity to decide what kind of activities they would enjoy participating in with you.

How do I communicate with them? The best way is to talk with them through telepathy (thoughts). This is typically the best way to communicate with spirits because the interaction is immediate. You can use tools like pendulums, tarot cards, automatic writing, scrying objects, etc and most collectors will use a mixture of tools before establishing what works best for them. Spirits can also initiate contact with you through telepathy, visions, and dreams.

Help! I can't see/hear/feel my spirits/spelled items, what do I do? The best and most important step you can take is to remain calm & not become frustrated or stressed because negative energy will simply exacerbate the situation. If you can find peaceful ground and exercise some patience you will see the doors open for you. When you have an agitated energy it makes it extremely difficult to make that necessary connection to open the doors for interaction with paranormal energy.

What language do spirits speak? Their own language native to wherever they lived. It's not uncommon for a spirit to speak their native tongue, but most of the time they communicate with you in your own, native language.

Where do spirit descriptions come from & can they look different to the Keeper than they do to the practitioners? The descriptions provided with a spirit come from the visual manifestation of the spirit during the conjuration process. It is possible they can appear in a different way to their Keeper, but unlikely. Usually spirits manifest how they wish to be seen by human Keepers and keep that form their entire relationship with the Keeper. There are times when Keepers have reported a variance in

Spirit Keeping: Q & A

appearance from description, but they are usually slight. Not all entities are capable of being understood by the human mind when in their true form, which is why they choose more human-like or human-comprehendible forms.

Why do some listings for spirits have long, detailed descriptions, and some do not? In the community of Spirit Keeping long-winded descriptions began on eBay. It is not typical that a practitioner should become overly involved in mingling with a spirit when they are intended to be re-homed. It can cause issues in the re-homing process as the only person who should bond with the spirit is the person the spirit is intended to be with as their Keeper.

Spirit interviews, spirit counseling, spirit communication services are all something that spawned from eBay and from those newer to the field, they aren't recommended practices because the only person who should be conversing with the spirits in your care is yourself, and in some cases when an issue does arise, the original practitioner should be the first consulted. With spirit consultation services it is too easy to open the door for intentional & unintentional false information. Those less honest will try to scare you into buying protection or services by telling you your spirits are bad. Some will try to tell you that you have the wrong spirits and you should only buy from "X" seller (someone they are in cahoots with). For those times when it is not intentional, false information from the spirit reader could be that the spirit you asked to be read doesn't want a third-party prying into their business.

For these reasons, and you can see how the issues can sprout further from the few mentioned, you should be the only one conversing with your spirits. Otherwise, you open yourself to more complications.

What if I don't feel anything from my spirits? What should I do? The best thing you can do is be consistent, be focused, and be dedicated to doing so. Sometimes people connect with a spirit immediately, within hours, some within months. It's difficult to say exactly when because each spirit

Spirit Keeping: Q & A

is different and you may connect to one spirit much faster than to another. Patience and persistence are going to be your biggest allies in making connections & bonding with spirits.

The most valued way to communicate is telepathy, but you can also use a communication board, pendulum, automatic writing, tarot, and many other outlets of a paranormal nature. Utilize any tools you can, including spells, associations, bonding rituals, and don't be shy to ask others in the community what their tips & tricks are, you'll find other Keepers are open, thoughtful, and great in sharing with other Keepers. Our forum is one such venue, and has thousands of threads for reference made by Keepers just like you.

Will my family or co-workers know my spirits are here? Likely not, unless you want them to. Spirits tend to keep to themselves unless they feel they are welcome outside of their Keeper. Spirits respect boundaries and will not manifest or interact with other members of your family unless you, or they, have given them permission to do so. This includes pets, who often sense and interact with spirits faster than humans do. With pets they may know something is there, but won't know what it is unless you give them permission to interact with your pets.

Q&A: Spirit Care

Do spirits need recharging? Typically spirits can derive this through exposure to natural cycles like the sun & moon. You can expedite this process through something like a Charging Box or a Charging Spell which provides a source of energy for the spirit to regain their energy to the fullest potential. Depending on the practitioner & method used to conjure & bind a spirit also depends on the approach you should utilize in providing your spirit energy. Speaking only for Creepy Hollows you can use the methods described above, for any other practitioner it is best to ask them if there are any restrictions in offering the spirits sunlight, moonlight, or enchanted methods of recharging energy.

Can vessels with a spirit be destroyed by water or sand? Typically, no. In the case of all Creepy Hollows offerings they cannot be destroyed or altered by water, sand, mud, salt, or any other mineral or compound. However, it is always best to err on the side of safety and ask this question to your practitioner of choice. Unless the practitioner tells you something specifically about your binding there is no substance that you are going to expose your vessel to that is going to harm, destroy, or otherwise mar the spirit or spell within.

What is a Charging Box? It is an object invented by Creepy Hollows which possesses the powers that energize the energy of a spirit or spell. It is not a necessity, but assists in an action that normally occurs over time. Charging Boxes are typically also used as a sanctuary for the spirit & their vessel.

How can I tell if a spirit has been recharged? If you are using a Charging Box most are completely effective within a few hours. If you are using the natural cycle of the sun & moon then your spirit will constantly be in a state of natural recharging.

Do I have to make offerings? No, you do not. Offerings can be made

Spirit Keeping: Q & A

out of respect & kindness if you want to show your spirit a kind gesture, but they are not necessary. If you do choose to leave them an offering or treat it is customary to leave it out for 12-24 hours. It is not something that has to be done all the time and only should be done when it is sincerely coming from your heart.

Are spirits safe around clearing rituals (sage, rituals)? All bindings we perform are, and most others are as well, but it is always the safest practice to check with the practitioner. Some less experienced practitioners may not have taken these actions into account in which case there could be some effect. Negative impact to the spirit in form of blockages, is most commonly felt through inadequate bindings subjected to banishing techniques.

What if I lose or break my vessel? Most practitioners will replace with a re-bind. For sellers who don't actually do the work themselves they can advocate for you to the practitioner they work with. Usually it is not a cause for concern and any spirit or binding can be recovered. However, in some cases it may pose an issue if the practitioner uses less than efficient methods.

Will having a broken or lost vessel hurt the spirit? Typically, no. Most practitioners do not have any stipulations that bond the energy of the spirit to the vessel in physical form; this is typically only seen with black magic. For most a broken or lost vessel is more an inconvenience for the Keeper than the spirit, and they can be bound to a new vessel by the practitioner.

What should I do with my spirits while I am on vacation? Leaving your spirits behind while you go on vacation is not a problem. They are well aware of what is going on and they aren't going to be traumatized by your absence. If your spirits are Bridged you can call them to you or send them to their vessel at will, which means it doesn't matter if you travel or not.

there are certainly some spirits who are better suited to being *Do spirits like having another spirit in the home who is a leader?* Typically, yes. Anyone likes to have a leader and a leader & organizer than others. It is not a bad idea to have a stronger personality in your group of spirits but be sure that you include the spirits in your home in the decision & respect them. You should always be the ultimate leader in your home, especially if you are dealing with DA entities or spirits. However, you can have a spirit in your home who is a trusted friend who is a leader on their own level as well. This should be a decision of mutual respect & understanding.

Spirit Keeping: Q & A
Q&A: Spirit Limitations

Do spirits need to be fed? No, they do not. They are in spirit form; therefore they are no longer in need of Earthen demands like eating, drinking, sleeping, etc. This should not be confused with an offering, which is giving a spirit something as a gift of friendship.

Can spirits be abused or harmed? The context of that expression denies itself. A spirit is a spirit therefore you cannot physically injure it. Are there nasty people in the world who have spirits to drag them down with themselves and be verbally abusive? Sure. Nasty people are everywhere but you have to remember we're talking about spirits. The spirit has the opportunity to move itself from the physical to spiritual plane at their own will. That is something you cannot take away from them no matter who you are, so if they are not liking a situation they are in they are going to move to the spiritual and/or astral plane.

People have to abandon the mind set that humans are superior beings. We are not, and we are graced by the presence of spirits, not the other way around. Spirits are far more advanced than we. If a spirit is permanently bound to a vessel and not attached, then they will likely go into the spiritual or astral realm and reside and not be with the vessel on the physical plane. Do not ever delude yourself that humans are more powerful than spirits or magic. That is a dangerous assumption & belief. Humans are privileged to practice magic & interact with spirits. This requires respect at all times since you are dealing with a force bigger than yourself. For most people they come into this Spirit Keeping world with honest intentions and that is what they receive in return... goodness & happiness.

Can spirits be forcibly bound? On any given day, no. Spirits are capable of holding their own against something trying to exact a malicious action against them. Binding is something that can only take place with permission; without permission the action

Spirit Keeping: Q & A

cannot be performed. A spirit is not a vulnerable weakling incapable of taking action to ensure their own safety & freedom. Permission is even required when a vessel is lost and a spirit needs to be transmuted to a new vessel, without it a practitioner cannot take action to move or re-home a spirit.

Can forcible binding happen ever? Yes, but you only see this in black magic practitioners who are summoning & conjuring Black Arts spirits or entities whose intentions as a whole are malicious. The majority of the people in the world do not hold the capability to force a superior being against its will. You typically only see this in black magic practitioners doing so against other Black Arts spirits to force them to do their bidding, because Black Arts spirits as a rule will not voluntarily help you.

However, it should also be noted that in this case the word "spirit" is inaccurate because most of the time the Black Arts "spirits" bound against their will are living entities who reside on another plane such as the astral or spiritual. And BA practitioners always pay in the end and you don't usually see their run last longer than a few months or a year before something breaks them down if they are going with the forcible approach. BA entities have powers beyond any scope of a human and typically a BA practitioner will allow themselves to become possessed by a strong BA spirit in order to continue BA work. The numbers of these kinds of practitioners are very few and far between.

Can you kidnap spirits? They are not vulnerable, unknowing beings floating around waiting to be taken advantage of. They require respect and often humility to bring them through conjuration and they choose whether or not to come to you. Your reciting a conjuration opens the gate for any spirit(s) who want to come forward to do so to you specifically. Think about the words being a key turning the lock on a door and when you're done the door opens to the spiritual or astral realms. You cannot do a spiritual drive-by and scoop up unsuspecting spirits. Spirits demand respect, rightly so, and you have to give respect to get it in anything in life including work with spirits.

Spirit Keeping: Q & A

Do spirits travel in families? 99% of the time, no. Is it impossible? No. Most of the time you will find spirits are singularly looking to be a part of someone's life; they are not living or existing in family units or packs as they are evolved past that point.

Can spirits procreate? Spirits do not have babies, they are spirits. They may have had babies when they were alive and they may go through those motions or relive those memories with you... and they may bring those other spirits into your life once they are settled but this is not the norm as stated above about spirit families. They do not usually bring others into an existing situation. As said before, there are exceptions to this, but the majority of the time you aren't going to have a spirit bring other spirits to you without your consent or knowledge. Respect & trust are a two-way street. You will see that spirits abide by respect & trust as so likely do you.

Do spirits get jealous, angry, or depressed? Typically, no. Spirits are evolved beings who have stepped out of their previous, mortal life and into the other side. They are not subject to the same hang-ups we as humans still experience. Have Keepers reported seeing this kind of behavior in their spirits? Yes, however the jury is still out on whether or not the Keeper is either projecting their own emotions into the situation or if humans are just incapable of appropriately processing some of the energies they feel from spirits and therefore are misinterpreting the situation.

Can spirits possess you? In the general sense that most people relate "possession" with? No. They are a spirit, not a living entity. The possessions you usually read about in religious literature are living beings, not spirits. Often the word "spirit" is used interchangeably with the word "entity" or the name of the entity which results in massive confusion. The translation of cultural texts & religious texts sometimes leads to these words being used inappropriately which results in inaccurate assessments of situations.

Spirit Keeping: Q & A

If you believe yourself to be possessed you should speak with a professional. There are many circumstances where possession is mistaken for something less severe.

How can more than one person own a binding of the same spirit? It's not usually common with the only exception being historic figures or celebrities. Of course the reason being more people are seeking them rather than the spirit seeking company with the person. A spirit binding is the binding of a spirit and not the soul. For that reason you can bind multiple aspects of a spirit. Think of it as taking slices from a pie; the whole pie is a pie and you have a piece of it which is constant and still a pie throughout.

Do spirits eat, get married, have babies, watch us in the bathroom, etc? No. They are in spirit form and are far beyond mortal desires. They were once living, have died, and become spirits. For this reason there is no need to do any physical tasks that human & some Earthen creatures do. Spirits do not wed because it is not necessary to do so; they aren't living in the same way you & I are living. They can't procreate in spirit form, some may have been able to when alive, but in spirit form they do not and there is no reason to; entities are dying all the time, they don't need to populate the spiritual realm. They don't eat, defecate, breathe air, breathe water, or any other physical action that sustains mortal life; they aren't mortal anymore.

Baby spirits sound very cute, but how do you take care of one? Do they grow or mature over time? No, baby spirits do not age, just as all spirits do not age. Once they have died from mortal form and become a spirit they are no longer subject to aging & death. They remain in the state they were when they died; especially with regards to their mental capacity. They are spirits, therefore they have more ability than we mortals, but they aren't as experienced, nor as developed, as those who lived a full life span and died. Adolescent and youthful spirits are distinctly different than adult spirits, and they can be more of a handful to care for because of their non-developed state.

Spirit Keeping: Bringing Spirits into the Home
Bringing Spirits into the Home

Inviting spirits into our homes is a personal matter. No one can tell you what is best for you, what will work & cohesively exist within your family structure. These are decisions that you have to make for yourself based on where you are in your journey and what makes sense for your life at the given time. You can derive direction from advice and get a sense of what others around you are doing, but each & every collector's journey will be different.

Let's start with some myths to clear the air. The first and most prevalent is that if you have spirits and you do not pay enough attention to them they will become angry or jealous. That's not true in the least. Humans are inferior beings to spirits who have already ascended & transformed to higher beings... or were born into ascension in the first place. While they can exhibit what we consider some "human emotions" they are far more evolved than we. Spirits are going to exist whether they are with you or not and being in a home where they can participate with its inhabitants (humans & other spirits included) is definitely a plus for them. They do not expect constant stimulation & attention from you. Spirits can go for months without interaction; some have gone thousands of years without it prior to being with you.

The second myth is you can have too many spirits. This is subjective. For some people one spirit is enough, for others, like me & Ash, there is no limit. We have literally hundreds and they have made colonies of their own in our home. Obviously we cannot spend time with all of them every day. We talk to them individually as well as in groups and this home has become a haven & sanctuary for them.

The third myth is if a spirit doesn't work for you right away it's not the right spirit for you. This is incorrect, in most cases.

Bringing spirits into the home isn't a method of solely enhancing

Spirit Keeping: Bringing Spirits into the Home

your life and having a subservient being to do your bidding. Bringing spirits into the home is a matter of companions complementing your life. Some spirits you feel drawn to may not manifest their purpose for being there for months or years. They can see into the future concerning their purpose for being with you, you cannot. They can see their purpose in your life whether it is immediate or 2 years down the road. For most collectors they find spirits enhance their life through at least companionship within the first few months of being home with you but their true purpose for being with you may not be realized for some time.

Collecting is a personal matter and each person will have their own journey. It is not about how many spirits you have; it's about who you feel drawn to and what their purpose is for being there. Naturally, people who are in stressful situations or in dire need of help will turn to magic & spirits, but it should not be the only reason for doing so. Absolutely nothing will happen if it is not meant as part of your path of destiny. Every single person on Earth would love to win the lottery; it is not in everyone's destiny and will not happen for you if it's not supposed to. If you work with magic or spirits, they can help you achieve a quicker or greater win, but if it's not in your destiny it will never happen. That doesn't just apply to the lottery, it applies to everything. We all have a main road of destiny that branches here and there as we exercise free will enough to temporarily alter our destiny but ultimately no matter how many side roads you take, you are still continuing a greater path you were meant for.

Bringing spirits into your home can be an incredible adventure. They come and go, in and out of your life as meant to. They are not tools for gaining wealth, power, beauty or fame only to be discarded once they deliver what you want. They have the power to bestow many rewards on your life, but they do so out of a mutual respect & relationship. There is no substitution for familiarity with your spirits. The success of Keeping is through time, not demand. Your life can be wholly transformed for the better but only as long as the proper respect is shown & they are not treated like tools for personal gain.

Spirit Keeping: Bringing Spirits into the Home

Having a variety of spirits in your home can also bring you a well-rounded complementary atmosphere. They each have their own strengths & abilities; it is not a cookie-cutter world in the realm of spirits. Different Gryphons will respond differently to you, different Djinn have different strengths & weaknesses, different Blue Dragons will have varying techniques and levels of Illusion. This is true across the board for all types of spirits. The importance of bringing spirits into the home is to decide why you are doing so. Is this because you have a passion for spirits and you are going to become a safe-haven for them? Or do you just want a companion & friend? Or because you are in the arts and want to give them a chance to work again? Is it any combination of these or something else entirely? You have to make that determination and of course things will change as time goes by but only you can decide what is true & right for you.

Spirits can work independently and they can work together. They will make their purpose for their presence known to you in the timeframe it is meant to be known. They are all companions to you, helpful & delightful in their own ways. They are also there to help with specific events which will be known when the event occurs. It's not about having one spirit that is your catch-all. A mega spirit who can cook, clean, wash the windows, do the laundry, watch the kids, dust the plants & grant wishes too. It's about complementing your life and enhancing it through the gift of spirits and giving them a purpose they would not have without you.

Spirit Keeping: How Many Spirits Should I Keep?
How Many Spirits Should I Keep?

This is a question many newcomers to collecting have. The answer is simple, as many as you feel you need in your life. Many seasoned collectors own a range of spirits through race and power. It is finding the right spirit that complements you and your life well that is the biggest task. No one wants to go into a home they don't feel welcome in and it isn't any different with spirits. You always want to bring spirits into your home that you feel you have a connection with.

The best thing to do is to look at your life presently and find out by keeping these spirits what is your goal? Do you just want someone to have fun with? A companion? A friend? Do you need help with something like family problems? Money? Love? Do you want to exercise paranormal and metaphysical powers? Psychic ability? Magic or enchantment? Become a spellcaster? Assessing your life is the single most important step in collecting.

Some have an intense passion for the spirits and want to exercise all aspects of this way of life. For those collectors you will find a very diverse family of spirits. Those interested in living the Spiritualist lifestyle typically have at least one of every major race of spirits: Fae, Angel, Immortal, Djinn, Creature, Dragon, and so forth. Because each race offers its own energy patterns and levels and they each have their own strengths with powers they find having a comprehensive collection the best way to experience a whole lifestyle. Collections do not happen overnight and Keepers typically collect as they feel motivated to grow.

Connecting with each spirit during the initial 30 days is important. It is not important to spend time with your spirits every single day after the initial 30 days. Once you've made a bond with your spirit they are a part of your life. They know you and are not going to become distant, upset or angry if you don't communicate with them every day. They know your heart, your

Spirit Keeping: How Many Spirits Should I Keep?

mind and your intentions. Especially with collectors who have large collections they allot time for their spirits and it may take a week or more to rotate between them. Being in your home, being a part of your life and sharing your time is more important to them than anything else.

There are activities you know certain spirits within your collection enjoy. Perhaps you take your aquatic spirits like Merfolk, Loxies, Nymphs, etc. in the bathroom with you when you shower so they can enjoy the steam. You take your fairies outside with you on nice days so they can enjoy being outdoors. You take your leprechauns with you when you go on nature walks or when you are going to interact with money (like going to the bank). Or you create special times like driving with your Dragons or going shopping with your Sterling Angels, etc. You'll quickly identify activities your spirits love to participate in!

The number of spirits you own can be limitless. What really matters is why you are collecting and that should be the main criteria for how many spirits you bring into your home.

What Should I Look For?

It is usually the opinion of unlearned people that in order to have something magical it has to be cast upon an antique vessel, high-priced jewelry, intricate tokens and other high-value items. That isn't at all the case and for those of us who are in the know we've seen spellcasted objects from multi-million dollar treasures to handkerchiefs.

From a marble to a thousand dollar ring any Spell, Spirit, Creature, Immortal, Dragon, Faery and such can be cast upon it or exist within it. Whether it be a shaman, witch, warlock, castor, sage, necromancer, or anyone else of the like. If you pay them they will cast on anything you want, even if it is a peanut shell and the spell they cast will work to its full potential regardless of what object it is cast on. If you live by the idea that only the beautiful and expensive things have powerful spells you will miss some great opportunities to own something spectacular.

The rule of "don't judge a book by its cover" applies to the paranormal just as much as it applies to everything else. Most people would be shocked to discover what paranormal things exist in their household without them even knowing, especially when you inherit family heirlooms or buy things from estate sales or antique stores. Sometimes the most powerful objects are simple, every day items. If you have means of detecting magical or paranormal objects in your home we suggest you take a moment to look around you and you will find surprises! There are no rules for what can be magical when it comes to the paranormal, you never know what you are going to find. Don't short change yourself, open your mind!!!

If a piece speaks to you then you should take a closer look. There are pieces meant for certain people and they will find you... just make sure you do not ignore the signs! There are a vast many treasures to be discovered... treasures that will change your life! They will become family heirlooms and no matter if it is a bead bracelet, gemstone, or an antique

Spirit Keeping: What Should I Look For?

you and those who own it after you will revel in its rewards and blessings. Open your mind and ears and listen for the calling for those treasures that are meant to change your life!

For spirits many Keepers describe it as feeling "the call". You should be careful not to be a trend follower; meaning bringing spirits into the home that have popularity or are the "in" thing. Spirit Keeping should involve you deciding what kind of Keeper you are; whether it's Keeping one or two spirits on a more close companion level, or keeping a large number of spirits who all contribute to one another in a community setting, or a vastly large number of spirits with multiple communities within your own home. The kind of spirits you keep and how many should be a direct result of what kind of Keeper you want to be. There's nothing wrong with being someone who has one or two, or someone like us who has large, spirit communities of hundreds of spirits, and most Keepers fall somewhere between.

The "call" from a spirit can be feeling something physically, emotionally, or mentally when you read their listing, or Encyclopedia article, or even when you think of the type of entity. Spirits can call you specifically by each, individual spirit, or an entire race can call you; then leading you to the specific spirit you are meant to be with.

Keep yourself open & be sure to be true to yourself; everything else will fall into place beautifully.

Spirit Keeping: Entities for a Specific Purpose

Getting Entities for a Specific Purpose; the Expectations & Outcomes

Expectation & outcome can be two different things, though usually with spirits they are providing you support & assistance in the best manner possible. Be sure you know the signs, from slight & impressive manifestations.

For example, if you want to keep entities who will provide you protection. What can you expect? This is a common question and one that you should fully understand before you buy an entity for protection. If a seller tells you that their entity will jump out and fight for you physically against a physical attacker no matter what, you need to close the listing or web page and keep going, as this is simply not the case.

This is not possible, at least not with any spirit that you are going to encounter on this realm. Anyone who tells you that no matter what happens, who it is, or where you are that your guardian will protect you against physical damage or death is a liar and I'm sorry to just come out with it, but it's true and as a collector you should know it!

I will try, to the best of my ability, to explain to you how a guardian or protective spirit works. Can they stop someone or something from hurting or killing you? Yes, they can. Will it be every time no matter what? No, it won't. You can't walk into a dark alley with dollar bills hanging out of your pockets and mouth off to a gang of shady characters expecting to survive because your Dragon, Gargoyle, etc. is going to come rescue you.

Recently a collector who has a Gargoyle wrote to me and said he was held up at gunpoint. He was confused as to why he was even held up if the Gargoyle is supposed to bring him protection. Here is my response to him and hopefully it will help shed some light on how guardians and protectors are used:

Spirit Keeping: Entities for a Specific Purpose

As with all guardians and protectors Gargoyles (and other entities meant for protection) cannot stop an action of destiny in motion but they can protect those involved in the action. Sometimes people get confused when I try to explain, so I will try to do this very simply. The man who held the gun to you was set in a path of destiny, he was meant to follow that line of destiny and there is little you can do from your end to interrupt his path. However, in that path if it could interrupt your path, such as shooting you as opposed to just pointing the gun at you, that you can stop. Unless you are a master at black or white magic you cannot alter or change someone else's path (and you don't want to because that makes you indebted to them) but you can stop yourself from being irrevocably damaged while they continue their path. Your Gargoyle can't stop his path, but he can stop someone from hurting you while they are on their path.

Or, for the person who wants to keep spirits who are known wish-granters? What can be expected for that? Too many new collectors have false notions of what can be obtained through wish-making. They read the fables of genies or spirits who brought their collector vast treasure inexplicably... such as millions of dollars, a mansion, a harem of women or men, etc. Objects that can render such results are guarded more closely than the crown jewels of England.

So what wishes do come true? Wishes that enhance the path of destiny you are on. Not to say there is only one path. The decisions you make every day affect the path you are on. You can change your path multiple times during the day; depending on how you live your life.

For example, if you go into work with a terrible chip on your shoulder and you are determined not to take stuff from anyone, you are on path 1 to ending your job. However, suppose once you get into work you lose your determination and decide to just live out a normal day, now you're on path 2. Then, someone steals your lunch and you lose your temper and scream at the co-workers around you. Now you could be back on path 1

Spirit Keeping: Entities for a Specific Purpose

or perhaps even a 3rd path. It is a simple example and I hope you understand its intent.

The wishes you make must enhance the path you are on or they will never come true. I can sit with my Star Faery all day and wish to look like Ava Gardner but I never will no matter how long I sit and wish. However, if I make a reasonable wish such as to gain enough money to make a vacation to Ireland... well, that wish will most likely be fulfilled.

No matter who you are or where you live you will never be able to wish something that doesn't exist in your life's path into existence. Many people quote lottery winners or winning gamblers and yes, it is true collectors have won thousands or millions of dollars... but, it was their life path and their wish for money manifested that way. Your wish for money may manifest itself in a few hundred dollars.

So will you ever have riches and wealth? Quite possibly... just not within a month, or a year. The wishes that you wish to come true may push you onto a path that will have great rewards and pay out in the long term, so don't discourage yourself from buying a wish-granting token because it won't yield you millions within a week. You can't wish the ridiculous into being true.

The same can be said of those who wish for their physical appearance to change. They want to know why they're still short, or why their crooked nose isn't straight, or why their eye color hasn't changed. The answer is quite simple... it won't happen. I hate to be straightforward and abrupt, but change to physical appearance is a skill you will never find through an object you find online through eBay or any other online venue. Those who have the power to change your physical appearance so drastically are those you are going to find sitting amongst the most prestigious individuals who practice magic and the odds of you ever being allowed audience in their sanctuary is slim.

However, there are changes to your physical appearance that can

Spirit Keeping: Entities for a Specific Purpose

transpire through the objects you find in general circulation; changes to your complexion, your weight, your hair texture, and your overall beauty. But, those who are looking to lose weight... do not expect to lose more than 20 pounds with a spell or enchanted object unless it is expressly made for those who can cast spells to help curb your appetite, stress level, metabolism and state of mind to bring weight loss over 20 pounds. Those individuals who claim such powers we suggest you interview with scrutiny. If you want advice on what you ask them feel free to write to us.

Every Keeper should keep a few spirits that have wish-granting powers. There are so many enhancements that can be made to your day-to-day life, but don't expect a shower of riches and wealth to fall upon you. Expect realistic wishes to come true and believe me, there are those wishes that can bring you the riches and wealth you want over time!

Getting Started

Now that you have brought them home you want to know how to get started. The best way to start is by greeting them, either out loud or through telepathy. Welcome them into your home just as you would any friend. Let them into your life, share the little & the big things, don't be shy to talk to them or ask their advice, and make them part of your life to the extent you feel comfortable with.

You can absolutely bond with multiple spirits at a time; you don't have to bond with one at a time. Some of us have hundreds of spirits in our care and we couldn't possibly spend time with each of them every day. They are going to talk with you via telepathy most of the time, and just like anyone you live with you aren't going to be engaged in conversation all the time, every day. Some spirits may be active daily, while others may be active weekly, or just when you need them; especially non-social spirits like Wraiths or Volkhs.

People who want to start collecting spirits come to do so in different ways. Some see a spirit, feel an immediate connection and feel drawn to start collecting... others find the literature before they find the spirits and they don't know where to start.

For beginners the best spirits to start with are Woodland Fae, Unicorns, Pegasus, Gnomes, Fylgias, and Angels. For youths the best entity to start with is a Unicorn.

Choosing the correct spirit is important. Before you go with any beginner recommendations you should go with the spirit that calls you as that will give you the best connection. However, if you want to start and haven't felt a calling in particular, any of the aforementioned spirits are a wonderful place to start.

Woodland Fae are eager to please, loyal, kind-hearted and their energy is easily felt by anyone new or seasoned.

Spirit Keeping: Getting Started

Unicorns are extremely loyal and can be a conscience for youths as well as a guardian. For adult collectors they find the Unicorns wisdom, generosity, patience and regal beauty an attraction. Unicorns are a must for any collection.

Pegasus are lively and likely to manifest as visions especially when the Keeper is in moving transportation such as a car, bus or train. They are also often heard on rooftops and their hooves heard on hard floors. They bring beautiful dreams and are well-loved by both their Keeper and other spirits in the collection.

Gnomes are grounded entities but can be a bit moody from time to time. They have a tangible energy and get close to family members. They do not leave once they make a connection.

Fylgias are wonderful guardians and protectors. Even newcomers can feel the guiding energy of Fylgias right away. They get close to their Keepers and enjoy keeping watch over them at all times.

Angels are sweet, joyful, loving entities that bring a bright light of positive energy and blessings to their Keeper's lives. They are easy to get along with and wonderful to interact with.

For those who want to dive directly into the Dark Arts it is advisable to acclimate yourself by starting with a spirit who is on the lighter side of the Dark Arts scale; such as Gargoyles, or Psy Vampires, or asking a practitioner if they have Werewolf, Djinn, or your chosen spirit on the lighter side of the Dark Arts spectrum. Working with Immortals can be advisable if they are on the gentler side. All Immortals are Dark Arts because they are living entities who have the capability of freedom of choice. Working with Immortals who are on the lighter side, such as Aphrodite or Sif, are good for helping you acclimate to Dark Arts energy and paving the way for more complex & intensive companions

Spirit Keeping: Getting Started

Newcomers are unsure how to prepare their home for their new friends. It is very easy. Secure a place in your home where you can keep your spirits when you're not able to bond with them. It can be a cleared place on a counter, dresser top, drawer, jewelry box, etc. This will be their sanctuary when you can't be near them.

It is suggested you spend at least fifteen minutes a day with them for the first 30 days they are with you and you keep their vessels near you at night, preferably no more than 1-5 feet from your bed.

To care for a spirit you must also care for the vessels they are in. The care of their vessels should be chosen wisely as to note cause any damage. If the vessel is made of solid silver or sterling silver you can use a silver polishing cloth to remove oxidation. Or, soap and warm water with a washcloth, paper towel, or soft toothbrush to remove debris. If the vessel is made of gold you can use a soft jewelry cleanser or soap & warm water with a washcloth, paper towel, or soft bristle toothbrush. If the vessel is made of wood, stone, ivory, or metal you can use soap and warm water with a washcloth, paper towel, or soft bristle toothbrush.

Do not be afraid to clean the vessels of your spirits if they are dirty or otherwise soiled. Keeping their homes safe, secure, and clean is important to their energy levels. If they are neglected or ignored they will not be as responsive as they normally would be.

If your vessel is a ring that is too small or too big, you can resize without danger to the spirit as long as you place them with a jeweler you trust. If you received a vintage vessel and it came to you missing stones or embellishments it is not a big deal, but if you lose more than 1 or 2 additional stones or pieces once you come to own the vessel it is important to replace and repair what has been lost.

Spirit Keeping: Getting Started

If your vessel has a crack or break it is important to repair the vessel to the best of your ability. Remember that spirits are completely aware of your heart and your intentions. If you cannot afford a proper repair and you fix it to the best of your ability your spirit will know your loving place of heart and that is what is important.

Most practitioners, like us, will obtain permission from both you & your spirit, and re-home them in a new vessel; if the vessel is lost or broken beyond repair. Because this happens to everyone we usually perform this service at no cost; exceptions being if the person wants a more expensive vessel than originally used.

Giving your spirits treats of food, music, poem, or other enjoyments is a nice gesture and greatly appreciated by your spirits. It is important to give them the proper treats and you should reference what your spiritual entity enjoys.

If you have a Charging Box for them, or a special area you plan on keeping their vessels, show them their place in your home. It's not a bad idea to have some personal touch to the area whether it is nice linen, a bowl with an offering, burning incense or candle in a scent they are associated with, or any personal object you enjoy that you think they would enjoy too.

Charging Boxes aren't a necessity, but they can be a quick & efficient way of providing your spirits a sanctuary they can call their own corner in your home. We provide instructions on our website on how to make your own Charging Box. You can find them in our Encyclopedia (encyclopedia.creepyhollows.com). You can also place the vessels on any dish or box you like & place them in the moonlight when you feel they are waning. The moon has incredible refreshing powers that can boost the "spirit" of any spirit; White or Dark

Associations & Offering

Utilizing Associations when bringing a spirit home is a good idea. You can find the Associations to spirits in our Encyclopedia (URL on previous page). This includes the weekday, month, color, animal, scent, herb, planet, gemstone, and foliage their energy resonates to. There are Associations for specific entities, and there are general Associations that are shared by all entities within certain classifications.

Associations can be used to create a closer connection with the entity. By recognizing their associations with the Earth and Universe you can use any combination of these tools to create treats, rituals, and bonding exercises between you.

You can purchase candles, incense, cones, oils, sprays, etc scented with the Scent, Herb, or Foliage they are associated with. You can purchase statuary, paintings, prints, textiles, etc with the Color, Animal, or Foliage they are associated with and keep them in your home where the entity will see them.

To boost their presence and give them a natural feeding of Earthen core energy you can buy raw, polished or cut specimens of the Gemstone they are associated with. Place the gemstones where you keep their vessel or wear the jewelry with the gemstones when you wear the vessel.

To have peak results it is best to meditate, perform rituals, invocations or spells for the entity on the Weekday they are associated with. The Month they are associated with is a block of time to celebrate and show your appreciation for your entity!

Following is a breakdown of general classifications and their Associations. Because they are general and can work with all entities within that classification there aren't as many Associations as those for specific entities.

Angels
Color: Gold
Herb: St. John's Wort
Weekday: Sunday
Foliage/Scent: Banana, Watermelon

Creatures (White Arts)
Color: Blue, Purple
Herb: Elecampagne
Weekday: Tuesday
Foliage/Scent: Pear

Dark Arts
Color: Black
Herb: Horsetail
Weekday: Friday
Foliage/Scent: Plum

Djinn
Color: Purple
Herb: Lavender, Dandelion, Peppermint
Weekday: Saturday
Foliage/Scent: Cherry

Dragons
Color: Ivory
Herb: Sage
Weekday: Friday
Foliage/Scent: Orange, Strawberry

Fae
Color: Pink
Herb: Cornflower
Weekday: Thursday
Foliage/Scent: Apple

Gargoyles
Color: Green *Herb*: Arnica
Weekday: Friday
Foliage/Scent: Orange

Immortals
Color: White
Herb: Barberry, Peppermint, Vervain
Weekday: Friday, Saturday
Foliage/Scent: Apple, Kiwi, Pineapple, Strawberry

Nympho
Color: Red
Herb: Peppermint
Weekday: Friday
Foliage/Scent: Peach

Vampires
Color: Orange (Psy), Red (Sanguine)
Herb: Aloe, Silverweed
Weekday: Friday
Foliage/Scent: Banana

Spirit Keeping: Getting Started

Connecting with Spirits

Connecting to your spirits varies by the entity. You should always use your entities Associations (that can be found in each entity's description in the Encyclopedia) to their best advantage. If your entity enjoys a certain scent, offering, color, number or such you should use it in conjunction with the time you spend with your entity. There are common practices you can use to connect to your entities. We have also developed a system that uses Code Words, words that are specific to each race of entity and can be used to provoke a greater connection.

How will you use these?

You can use the code word(s) by

* speaking them aloud
* speaking them through telepathy
* writing them on paper and presenting it to the entity
* making the word(s) part of a conjuration, spellcasting, or ritual * any other way you deem fit!

There are countless ways you can implement the power of code words. You can use them to encourage contact with a spirit not very active, you can increase the power of a relationship between a spirit or entity and yourself, you can temporarily invoke a spirit to see what their energy is like, and many other invaluable uses!

By using the code word(s) you are making a gesture of good faith & good will; extending your energy to them for receptive interaction. This charts a pathway for exchange in terms of bonding, interacting, and experiencing the specific spirit or entity. Because of the time involved in creating proper, working, and powerful Code Words, we offer these for sale. However, there are plenty of free methods you can use to connect with your spirits.

Spirit Keeping: Getting Started

You can use any of the following invocations to connect to your entity. Hold the entity or have them within one foot of you while you recite any of the following. You can recite them as many times as you need and some find lighting candles helps to create the energy needed to make the connection.

This is an invocation you can use with any Angel race.
ANGEL INVOCATION
Winged friends of ethereal bliss
Open your gilded arms in commune
Allow me audience with you in friendship
To bond and know each other in ways of kindred
Welcoming all that is new & right

This is an invocation you can use with any Creature race.
CREATURE INVOCATION
Gentle friends who are guardians of time
Know that I seek your guidance & friendship
Extending loyalty, truth, and honor
To be your fellow companion & humble ally
Let me know the treasured counsel you provide
As my respect for our alliance is greatly expressed
Through my humble actions and request
I give thanks that you consider me
In this plea for your guidance
Opening new doors for me

This is an invocation you can use with any Dark Arts race. **DARK ARTS INVOCATION**
Those who live on the invisible line
I know the decisions you bear each day
Allow our commonality to be a binding force
Appreciation & gladness to know someone like each other
And the will of my spirit!
Drawing us closer in our pursuit of companionship

Spirit Keeping: Getting Started

This is an invocation you can use with any Djinn race
DJINN INVOCATION
Born of the special blood
Your responsibilities extend across multiple realms
Powers exceeding any expectation conceivable
Allow my petition to be heard
That we work in harmony to achieve wishes & desires
Provide me guidance, support, and your favor

This is an invocation you can use with any Dragon race
DRAGON INVOCATION
Beauty still is the night and come forth
Sail the moon and stars for your destination
Is with me, here and today, for eternity
I beckon to you with the calm of my heart
And the will of my spirit!

I call to you as friend and beloved
That you may find solace & home with me
You are an inspiration and joy to my life
I call you because you are needed
Because you and only you can help

Come to me my dragon of desire
Come and make my life more fulfilled
For I call you now as a companion So that we may share, enrich & enliven
Each other for all the days to come!

This is an invocation you can use with any Faery race
FAERY INVOCATION
A sweet and happy day for us to share
A joy of blissful life comes to me with your presence!
You are a true and loyal friend
I rejoice in knowing we will be together
To share and live our lives as friends and confidantes
You are a ray of sunshine that shines upon me and brings excitement to my life
I am sincerely humbled by your company!

This is an invocation you can use with any Gargoyle race.
GARGOYLE INVOCATION
Lift the stone from your lungs, dear friend
And take in the air of kinship around you
I am here that you may find comfort in our companionship
Two, unto each other, as friend and siblings of spirit
I call thee unto my side for eternity
That we may know each other and find grand likeness in life
I speak your name so that you know I call you as my own
I invite you as part of my life, (say name)

This is an invocation you can use with any Immortal race
IMMORTAL INVOCATION
The sun and moon rise to bring a glittering star
A star that will carry the purpose and will
Of this great Immortal
Smile and carry on gilded wings your help
I call to you as you are filled with power
To grace upon me with a humble nod
The gifts that you behold as acknowledgment
Of my admiration and enjoyment of your presence
I accept your gifts with a happy heart
Come to me oh (name of Immortal)!
Come to me and I will give you a sanctuary
Where we can dwell and learn together.

Spirit Keeping: Getting Started

This is an invocation you can use with any Nympho.
NYMPHO INVOCATION
Come to me playful companions of ecstasy
Let us enjoy the romp of desire & passion
Clinging to one another in an intimate embrace
Sharing a bout of raw sexual power & energy
Wrapping ourselves in the hot & sticky tendrils of sensual ascension of mind, body, & spirit

This is an invocation you can use with any Sanguine or Psy Vampire race.
VAMPIRE INVOCATION
Wet your lips fair one
Find the stretches of your energies here
Paw the night's moon and shadows
Let the races of your mind find you
I summon your presence
Come and let us share the abyss of eternal time
Come to me now (say name) and reveal yourself

GENERAL INVOCATION
(Can be used with any spirit; White or Dark)
I call to thee oh spirit of enchantment
I call thee to this token of sacrifice
As it will serve as a home and sanctuary for you.
You will find a friend of loyal and true blood in me and I in you.
I call you and will that you be bound in love to this token
You are welcomed and cherished forever
You are beckoned as you are the true answer.

Spirit Keeping: Getting Started

Meditating with Spirits

If you want to make connections with your spirits on a deeper level meditating is a great way to make that bond. Be sure that you have the vessel of the spirit you want to connect to with you before you start.

The best way for beginners to meditate is to start by allotting fifteen minutes of solitary time - without noise, TV, phones, family or any other distraction. Some find using soft music, candles, incense or other atmospheric tools useful in setting the appropriate energy for meditation.

It is not necessary that you sit in an erect posture, such as a Yoga position, in order to meditate. You can sit in your favorite chair, lie on the floor, lie on your stomach, or use any position of relaxation that suits you best. Relax your mind, clear it of any plaguing thoughts from the day. Let your body go limp, do not have tension in your joints or muscles, completely relax.

Some prefer to have their eyes closed, others to keep them open... whatever works best for you. If you're not comfortable and in the proper frame of mind meditation isn't going to work for you.
Once you feel you are in the zone of relaxation hold the vessel in your hand, place it on your chest, hold it between both hands,
and place it on your closed eyelids, on the top of your navel...
whatever is most comfortable for you as any of these choices   work.

You can start by just having a conversation with the spirit
through telepathy. Let the spirit know you are welcoming them to come through to you in whatever method they deem fit and concentrate on the center of your forehead as you do this to help open your third eye channel and make a stronger connection.

Repeat this method of meditation at least 5-15 minutes a day

Spirit Keeping: Getting Started

for the first 30 days. The time of day isn't important, whatever time best fits into your schedule because you will need complete quiet.

The more you meditate the more you will come up with the methods that are most active for you and the length of time you meditate with likely lengthen as your communications with your spirits grow more and more.

There is no wrong way to meditate. When your heart and mind are in the right place and you are truly welcoming your spirit to join you then you can't go wrong!

Altars/Sanctuaries

Usually people associate altars with a place where something is worshipped. We aren't worshipping spirits, so in the case of reference to Spirit Keeping an altar is more of a personal sanctuary that you enjoy and a place you can enjoy with the spirits in your keep. Some who also practice magic may have dual-purpose altars, but for Spirit Keepers your personal space is for you to enjoy with your spirits.

Typically a sanctuary area will include a nice linen, a few offering bowls to make offerings to different spirits, incense, candles, vessels of the spirits, any Charging Boxes, and any personal touches you wish to make.

If you have limited space, you can make multiple offerings in the same bowl; doing so isn't an issue and doesn't pose any confusion or problem. The spirits know which offering is for them.

For those who have limited space or are on the go often you can keep an altar/sanctuary box where you unpack & pack these items to use as needed. Typically, it is recommended that you spend at least 15-30 minutes a day with your spirits, but you don't always have to do that in your sanctuary space.

Just making them part of your life & talking to them throughout the day is just as good, if not better.

Tips, Tricks, & Tidbits

Because every spirit is different you are likely to find your own tips & tricks when it comes to connecting & what different spirits in your keep enjoy. These are some universal tips, tricks, & tidbits we've found in our years of Spirit Keeping.

Vampires, both Psy & Sanguine, love and go crazy for Aloe. You can use it in a lotion, soap, or spray on yourself for connection... buy an aloe plant for the house and break open the leaves for offerings... or buy any form of aloe to place near their vessels.

Dragons love sea glass; they enjoy it as bedding or an offering. They are also crazy about fruit; any scent, spray, fresh, dried, candle scent, etc.

Fae love shiny objects; mirrors, gemstones, or glass. They love to be surrounded by decadent & beautiful things. They have a great appreciation for art & for the beauty of nature; including flowers, trees, shrubs, and herbs which you can use as offerings.

Elves are stoic; they usually view themselves as guardians of nature. They believe in living off the land and using everything you take. For that reason making offerings of anything from nature is best if it is being re-purposed or used for something other than an offering to them.

Djinn adore lavender and respond highly to any form of lavender they are around. Using lavender when you are making a wish to the Djinn amplifies the connection & energy between the two of you; thereby making the request a greater experience. Making offerings of lavender at any time will increase the Djinn's energy around you. You can also

Spirit Keeping: Getting Started

use lavender-scented soap or lotion on yourself to increase your physical energy-bond to them.

Nymphos are best engaged when you have already started sexual action. If you want to connect more quickly to your Nympho it is best to start the action yourself and invite them into it. They are spirits that derive complete energy & pleasure from sexual action. Therefore, engaging in it is the best way to connect to them.

Angels are very ethereal, and their energy is spiritual. Engaging in spiritual activities such as yoga, tai-chi, meditation, astrology, star-gazing, religious reading, etc will boost the kind of energy they respond to and therefore boost the bond
between the two of you.

Will Spirit Keeping Work for Me?

This is question that haunts the minds of all newcomers. The answer to that question lies with you. Not everyone can see, hear or communicate with spirits. Sometimes it is just a matter of energy make-up and sometimes it is just the non-belief that these things exist. Humans are extraordinarily unique and so not everyone will experience Spiritualism on the same level.

Some people are born with a natural gift of psychic nature or medium powers to speak to the dead. Some have a natural affinity for the mystical and spiritual and therefore seek out this lifestyle.

One thing is certain you are reading this right now for one of two reasons:

1. You love the mystical and want to learn more about it so you can practice it for yourself or
2. You are just curious. If you are here for reason #1 then you are already on the right path towards becoming someone who can keep and interact with spirits.

If you are someone who naturally is drawn to the spiritual, metaphysical or paranormal then keeping spirits is going to be easy for you and something that you'll tremendously enjoy. Being a Keeper brings gifts, rewards and powers beyond your wildest dreams and they positively impact your life forever.

Spirit Keeping: A Guide for Spirit Keepers

It is impossible to tell you step by step exactly how a spirit is going to react with you when everyone is different. As long as you are willing to put your best foot forward you will find that the spiritual world will welcome you.

Help! I Can't Feel My Spirit!

This is a common phrase uttered by collectors of novice to well-seasoned and is a natural occurrence that happens to everyone.

There could be multiple reasons you are not feeling your spirits and the chance that they have left you, abandoned you or otherwise dissipated is less than 1%. To start with, spirits can not leave a vessel or soul once they are bound. From here on the word "vessel" will encompass both a physical object and/or being bound to a human's spirit.

Spirits do not have free will to change vessel or abandon a vessel at whim. They are eager to be given a home and find it as their personal sanctuary and safe haven. They are not going to up and abandon their shelter any more than you would abandon your home. They cannot leave their vessels to go to other people or other places. While it is possible they can be sent on errand for you to help another person they cannot make that decision by themselves. If you ask them to give aid, comfort or other assistance to a friend, family member or stranger and they have the ability to do so then you may feel a temporary absence during their time helping the person you specified but they cannot decide to take leave of you by themselves.

The odds that someone powerful enough, and with enough skill, will choose to steal your spirit(s) from their vessels is less than a 1% chance. Any reputable conjurer/practitioner will bind the spirit with a protection invocation as part of the binding process limiting drastically the chances that the spirit can be unwillingly removed from their vessel.

The reasons you may not be feeling your spirit(s) could be a change in your energy... a drastic swing from happy to sad, taking medicine or changing dosages of medicine, or on the more unpleasant side having bought from a fake practitioner, having a hex, curse or evil eye placed upon you.

Spirit Keeping: Help! I Can't Feel My Spirit!

If that is the case the removal of said hex, curse, etc will allow your spirits to contact you again and that can take anywhere from 24-96 hours after it is removed. There are ways to protect yourself by owning at least one entity for protection, though multiple entities are recommended.

However the simplest reason, and most common, is just a change of energy. Perhaps you're not getting as much sleep as you used to, you have had a life change (new job, newborn, moved somewhere new, breakup, divorce), drastic change in diet, and these are temporary energy changes that will straighten themselves out. These kinds of blockages are normal & usually remove themselves. If they do not, the best thing you can do is utilize your favorite cleansing & refreshing routine be it smudging, having a "you" day to rejuvenate, or having a cleansing or clearing done for you (by a professional or an enchanted vessel).

It could also be that you are not a naturally sensitive person and have a more difficult time achieving contact with the paranormal. So don't worry! With patience, focus and determination to try your best you will find yourself in contact.

For those who want more reassurance there is one method that tends to work far more than any other. There are a few tried and true methods, though invoking a spirit to appear when they don't want to never really makes them happy. This method tends to work with them more often, but if the spirit doesn't want to show themselves, they won't.

Mirrors are extremely powerful tools when trying to conjure spirits (hence the games kids play like Bloody Mary, etc.) If you want to invoke a spirit I suggest you settle yourself mentally before you begin because what appears to you in the mirror may startle you even if what appears isn't grotesque. However, my husband has conjured spirits this way that gave me nightmares for 3 days. But, if you are working with what is supposed to be a white spirit, it won't be bloody, gory, or scary, but it might be startling.

Spirit Keeping: Help! I Can't Feel My Spirit!

Either stand using a bathroom or vanity mirror or if you want to use a smaller mirror place it on the floor and sit down directly in front of it leaning over into the mirror. Now, some people turn off the lights and use candles... it does help set the atmosphere but it is not necessary.

Place the object with the spirit in your hands or if it is too big place it in front of the mirror. This works every time with human spirits and may take a few tries with other entities.

Once in front or over the mirror recite (this is only the invocation for white/positive energies):

Little friend in my looking glass come out to play
I ask you be a companion haunting me today
Show your face little friend, let me see you shine
I am your beholden and you, dear friend, are mine

Immediately you should see something in the reflection. You can try this as many times as you want if you do not get results the first time. You are not going to damage anything by doing this multiple times.

If you're having trouble contacting, interacting, or communicating with your spirits there's no reason to worry! We can help you every step of the way to develop a communicative relationship with your spirit companions.

Many new Spirit Keepers can have questions about how to interact & communicate with their new spirit companion. Spirit Keeping can be a very rewarding experience that can enhance your life in many ways. We are always here if you have questions through Support or our Forum.

These are the best recommendations for those who who are having trouble and are the best places to start!

Be sure to read our articles 9 Things You're Doing Wrong as a Spirit Keeper, The 5 Stages of Spirit Keeping, and What Kind of Spirit Keeper are You? in our Encyclopedia for more information.

Open the Door to Spirit Communication

First, think about the spirit you feel the closest to. Which spirit do you immediately think of when reading this sentence? This should be the spirit you start with. You will find that if you can get your foot in the door with communication & interaction with a spirit then it makes it far easier to recognize and realize interactions with other spirits.

Second, once you have the spirit (or even more than one spirit if you feel multiple connections) you can then begin to forge the bond that will open the door to spirit communication. You can use any and all of the techniques below. If you'd like you can try one at a time until you feel the connection or you can try all the techniques below at the same time. There isn't a right or wrong answer, the goal is for you to be able to feel your spirits.

- Introductory Invocation
Invocations are not necessary with CH bound spirits, but if you feel you aren't sensitive enough to interact and engage the spirits around you then this can be useful for stimulating your spiritual energy and making it easier for you to interact.

You can recite this out loud or via telepathy:
Welcome friend I cherish thee
Open my eyes so I can see
Your companionship I value dear
To me never be shy to appear

- Tasking
Spirits want to help you, they want to interact with you, that is why they wanted to come to you. If you give them something to help you with they will gladly participate to reach the goals you desire.

In the beginning, even if you don't think anyone is listening (they are), before you start your day give your spirits something they can help you with. Even if it's something simple like, "I don't feel well today, please give me some uplifting energy", or "My co-worker Jane is annoying me, please keep her from making me crazy today", etc. Tasking your spirits helps them to be interactive with you and therefore you have a greater chance of feeling them and realizing their contribution to your daily life.

- Manifestations
This one is important. It's vital that you do not pigeon-hole your spirit manifestation expectations. Spirits can manifest in hundreds of different ways. They can manifest through thoughts, as orbs of light, as streaks of light, as Shades (out of the corner of your eye),

as temperature variances, as phantom sounds or phantom scents, in your dreams, and even in dreams they can appear in various forms, not always their true form.

This is the single most troublesome issue for Spirit Keepers who say they can't feel/see their spirits. You have to recognize even the most subtle of signs because this is vital to your ability to realize spiritual energy and work with spirits moving forward.

- *Consistency & Patience*
DO NOT GIVE UP. I know it's easy to get discouraged but you have to remember your spirits chose to come to you. They selected you out of the thousands of other people they could have chosen to be with. Make it a habit to talk to your spirits every morning, even if you just say "hello" to all of them and share some of your thoughts for the day. The same at night, say a "goodnight" to all of them and have a few, brief thoughts to share.

Don't let stress, worry, and anxiety creep into your experiences. These are the 3 most common killers for feeling & interacting with any paranormal experience whether it's spirits or spells.

How-To Protect Your Spirited Vessels

Any practitioner of any level will tell you that protection of the work they've done is of the utmost importance. You do not want what you have created to be used by others
without your permission. Certainly if you were to lose an enchanted or spelled piece you do not want someone to be able to unlock its secrets. Sometimes you do not want someone
to even know that what you possess contains anything more than the material it is made of.

This section provides you with a free Dead Spell. A Dead Spell is a Creepy Hollows original to make the magic, enchantments, spells or spirits contained within an object to go
"dead" whenever someone without your permission touches it or comes near it; they are only active to you and anyone else you grant permission.

Anyone who finds your pieces, steals your pieces, or tries to uncover the secrets of your pieces will not be able to. They will sense and find only a "dead" vessel.

This is invaluable and can be used with any White or Dark Arts spirit. You can use it on as many pieces as you wish and it will not harm, lessen the power of or otherwise detract
from the bindings in any way. It only prevents outsiders from being able to tamper with what belongs to you.

To prepare, I always suggest using a cleansing spell because it never hurts the spells or spirits and only cleanses the vessel or location from any natural, negative energies.

Spirit Keeping: How-To Protect Your Vessels

Spell to use to cleanse the object & prepare it for casting:
With the tides of spiritual energy
Wash away the plaguing binds
Prepare this space for great magic/spirits
To be received & bound eternally
A clean canvas for gifts to be given

After you cast the Cleansing spell allow the vessel to sit for 5-10 minutes before proceeding.

Now you are ready to apply the Dead Spell to your vessel so others will not know the powers of your vessel. You can also cast this on yourself to make any spirits or spells you have bound directly to your spirit undetectable by anyone unless you give them permission.

The Dead Spell
Great bindings find a shield to guard you
Hidden from the searching light & prying eyes
Cloak yourselves in these words of ancient protection
Ibyan mosetro eben (Eh-bee-an, moh-set-row, eh-ben)

The moment you finish speaking this spell it is bound.

If you want to reverse the spell and make it so anyone can detect your spirits you will need to prepare a bowl of water seasoned with fresh rose petals. Leave the fresh rose petals in the bowl of water overnight before using or casting. I suggest casting the bowl of water in case you are going to use it for multiple vessels. Place a dab of the seasoned water on the vessel and leave it overnight to have the spell reversed.

Reversal spell words:
Gisaya ovtro medem
(Gee-say-ah, oh-voh-tro, may-dem).

Spirit Keeping: The Well-Rounded Collection

The Well-Rounded Collection

Before you do anything else you must make some determinations about yourself. Are you someone who is best suited for spirits, enchanted vessels, or both? Are you open to white, dark or both?

What are the pros & cons of each for you? Make a list; it's an effective tool for figuring out what you really want. To start at the top of the list write a sentence, paragraph or keywords regarding what you are looking for in collecting; is there a specific purpose you want to fulfill or are you going to be a die-hard, paranormal collector?

Spirits often require a relationship between Keeper & Spirit. Relationships can be very rewarding for those who want an interactive lifestyle and want another being to actively participate in their life. Spirits manifest in many, many ways providing feedback, guidance, wisdom, companionship, powers & assistance. However, for someone who does not feel they have the time or does not want to make that kind of personal investment it may be better for them to take a path of enchantments & spells only. Spells & enchantments can often accomplish the same efforts as Spirits without the personal relationship. If you are someone who is an optimistic, uplifting, sweet personality it is unlikely you will feel a draw towards the Dark Arts.

The Dark Arts encompasses a far wider range of Spirits than White Arts because the term "Dark Arts" doesn't mean evil or foreboding. It simply means a being that has the capability of deciding to be good or bad... just like you, me and any human. Many Dark Arts Spirits are helpful, generous, good beings that can provide a lot for you but they will have mood swings from time-to-time just as any human. You may at least want to investigate having a Dark Arts Spirit such as Wraith for protection in your home since Wraiths are an extremely low-maintenance, keep-to-themselves sort of beings. However,

Spirit Keeping: The Well-Rounded Collection

Dark Arts, even at its lightest, is not for everyone.

Another misconception is that if you are looking for Psychic Power, Wealth, Astral abilities, etc. that one piece with the powers you want will fulfill your desires completely. That is not true. We collect multiple pieces of every aspect we want because each casting will have its own strengths & its own capabilities, especially when you are talking about different cultures in magic.

For an example, if you have 2 different pieces both cast with Psychic Power spells they will work towards the same goal (Psychic Power) but they will go about it in different ways. Where one is weaker the other may be stronger and vice versa. It is because the spells used to enchant the piece will have their own strengths and will respond & behave differently than each other while still providing you your ultimate goal of gaining Psychic Power. Not to mention a Psychic Power piece with French spells will have its unique energies & responses to an African Psychic Power piece. You will find that in different situations that one amulet works better for you than another. It doesn't make one better or worse, it means that the more well-rounded collection you have the more you will experience, learn and grow.

This is the same for any enchanted piece whether it's for Good Luck, Wealth, Love, Healing, Divination, Astral Power, Magic, Cleansing, anything! We recommend at the bare bones having at least 3 pieces of each enchantment that you desire to work for you. They can be of varying classes or intensities and recommended to be of different cultures or genres of magic so you can experience all there is available to you. Of course the more you have of different aspects the more experiences and varying results you will have.

This works the same for keeping Spirits! All Angels aren't alike just as all Vampires, Dragons, Immortals, etc. aren't all alike. They each have their own specialties, their own strengths and your experiences with each will be different, sometimes

Spirit Keeping: The Well-Rounded Collection

drastically different. You may find that you respond a lot better to one race of Spirit over another and that is not unusual. Many collectors find that they respond better to one over another and while they enjoy having varying races of Spirits around them the ones they are the closest to are those they find they have more intense relationships with. It is not entirely unknown or impossible for you not to connect with a particular race of Spirit at all; that happens too. Use your best judgment when it comes to not connecting with a Spirit. Before you give up make sure there isn't any other situation present that would prohibit you from making the connection, impatience is nary a virtue in the world of the paranormal.

Dark magic vs. White magic draws a far clearer line than Dark Arts Spirits vs. White Arts Spirits. Dark magic is intended to absolve the person being cast upon of their free will, whereas White magic influences a person in a direction without absolving their free will. Dark magic is not easily cast and not always rewarding. Dark magic, even when cast with good cause, can affect your karma and the unseen, written record. While Dark magic may accomplish what you are set out to do it could also end up costing you a lot more than you intended to pay. If your Dark magic not only affects the person intended to be the recipient but also injures an innocent person in its wake you are held liable & responsible for the innocent party being injured. When Dark magic is not cast properly it can also come back on the initiator. Which means even if you are not the caster but the one who requested it you are the source & you are the one who will receive the backlash.

If you insist on using Dark magic be sure you are doing so responsibly and working with a professional who knows what they are doing. White magic can often accomplish what you need done without the injury to your spirit & karma. It influences a person or situation with your desired outcome. It doesn't rob anyone of their free will and allows what you want to happen by shaping a path of destiny. Destiny is a like a large tree... it has a straight point from root to top but it has many branches along the way. When you influence something to happen it is like

Spirit Keeping: The Well-Rounded Collection

taking a detour onto a branch, ultimately you will be back on the straight line from the root to the top but in the mean time you are enjoying being "out on the limb" so to speak!

However, when you start talking about Love spells or other spells that can affect not only your destiny but directly impact the destinies of others that is when you can see spell results start to vary drastically. Sometimes, no matter how much you want something to happen and no matter how many times you cast or how much money you pay for them to be cast, the spell will never have your desired result. In cases where a spell is cast to not only affect you but others as well we recommend that you have it cast or cast it yourself 3 times within a maximum of a 90-day window & see what results take place from those 3 castings within 30 days of the last casting.

If absolutely no results occur do not continue to throw money at the situation, let it rest for awhile and try again at a later date. That may be hard to hear but sometimes it is not the lack of skill of a caster (that is why we recommend 3 castings preferably by 3 different casters even if you are 1 of the 3), sometimes it is just not going to happen. It can be a difficult situation when spellwork is entangling multiple lives at once. Overall and above all else use your best judgment. Really feel good about a choice whether it is Spirits or Spells. Trust your intuition and if you feel you need some support truly seek out the community for answers too; sometimes a second or third opinion when you are having trouble can be a good thing.

Every single one of you is going to have your own unique path, no two are ever alike, so do not strictly go by someone else's results as indication of how your results will be with the same Spirit or Spell. We're here for you, the members of the forum are here for you and so are many other practitioners & collectors worldwide! Having a healthy, well-rounded collection can really make a big difference for you.

Do not feel this is going to happen overnight either. For some it may

Spirit Keeping: The Well-Rounded Collection

happen sooner than later but sometimes a good, well-rounded collection can take years to build as you find what responds to you and what calls you. Patience! Do not be in a rush, all good things will come to you!

As you grow in your journey, if you feel there are pieces you have outgrown or are not right for the path you intend to take you can offer them to other collectors via the Marketplace as well so do not feel that you are locked into where you are now. Although it is necessary for you to realize that even though you are not on a certain road today, you may be next year or even next month.

Enchanted vessels with Spells will keep forever and Spirits are not common-beings, they have surpassed a mental level that humans cannot begin to comprehend. They are not going to be angry, jealous, injured or hurt if you tell them that now is not the right time for the two of you. They can outlast any human with patience. Again, use your best judgment and make the decisions you believe are right for you, not just because someone else tells you it's right.

The Dark Truth

Dark Arts are often misunderstood and it likely has to do with the fact that Dark Arts encompasses a vast variation from human to pure evil. Dark Arts simply means the ability to choose & do good or bad. This is why humans & many Dark Arts entities fall into the lighter side of the Dark Arts spectrum. As humans we have the ability to choose right or wrong; we can do a good thing or a bad thing. For most of us we choose to do right, we choose to try and live our lives with some expectation of not hurting or causing harm to others. This is the same for most Dark Arts entities.

However, descending down the spectrum into what most people conceive as Dark Arts lay the races of beings & entities that could care less about the pain of others and will fight not only amongst themselves but against anything that stands in their way... and some just for the pure pleasure of causing pain. There are many races that fall into this class including dark races of Angels, Demons (Stuhac, Dybbuk, Hitotsume-Kozo, etc.), Watchers, Dragons (Bolla, etc.), and Destructors (Blemmyes, Bukavac, Clurichaun, Each Usige, etc.).

It is crucially important for you to understand the difference between who should technically be labeled "Grey Arts" (the human race & many Dark Arts races) and "Black Arts" (beings & entities who enjoy evil). Knowing & understanding the difference between these is vital in keeping your home safe. Any of the entities in the Encyclopedia for which we do not supply associations and say "not recommended for keeping" are those who fall into the Black Arts.

A myth that has circulated since good & evil began is that the Dark Arts are stronger than White Arts. That is not true and prejudicial for the fact that Black Magic recruits those who are in a desperate state of mind. Often humans find themselves in situations they consider dire. They want, at any cost, the

Spirit Keeping: The Dark Truth

outcome they desire, such as getting a boyfriend or girlfriend back even though that may not be the best idea. Humans are easily clouded by emotion & tunnel vision. Some do not take the time to open their eyes to the bigger picture. If someone is meant to come back to you then you would be able to accomplish the task with either Black or White magic. That is what is seldom said but a concrete truth. If something is truly meant to be and is in *your* best interest you would be able to accomplish the effort through Black or White magic because it would conform to your path. However, if you want to force something to happen, ripping away the other person's free will, you can accomplish anything through Black magic, but at a price.

That is what separates Black Arts & Black Magic from White Arts & White Magic... free will. You will find that black magic & white magic spells follow a similar path for awhile with love spells, justice spells, wisdom spells, etc. The path splits when Black Magic turns into sacrificing either *your* free will or someone else's free will. To many who are uneducated in the area they will not see the truth behind the promised outcome. The truth being it will come to you at a steep price. Yes, you may get back your love or you may cause harm to someone who hurt you but you are unaware of the invisible price tag hanging from it and what will haunt you the rest of your mortal life (if not into other lives as well).

Black Magic has a place in the paranormal world just as deservedly as White Magic. Black Magic & White Magic can stand toe-to-toe but what makes White Magic stronger than Black Magic is that conquering White Magic is a much more difficult road than Black Magic. For humans who want immediate help it is easier just to be bad, lazy or uncaring than to be compassionate, and work hard for something.

The power of counterbalance is the strongest power in the world and NEVER let anyone tell you otherwise. Anyone who does not realize that the balance of White Magic & Black Magic

Spirit Keeping: The Dark Truth

in perfect unison is the most powerful force in any universe is ignorant of the truth. There is no stronger force in the world. Black Magic exists as a push against White Magic & White Magic the counterbalance to Black Magic. Those who can use the Black Arts in harmony with the White Arts can conquer both fields of battle. However, this is the most difficult unison to obtain.

For many you will choose to stay with either White Arts or Grey Arts (Dark Arts), or both, and that is perfectly okay. Even some of you will choose a path of Black Arts and to you I say travel lightly. There is nothing wrong with opting to stay in the light of the White Arts or in the lighter side of the Dark Arts, that is why all of us are different and we need that mixture of people to counterbalance those who choose only the path of Black Arts. Again, without balance there is a problem. So for most of you the power of Unison (Black & White Arts) is knowledge, and since knowledge is power it will aid you.

That is the Dark Truth of the Dark Arts and hopefully it has helped some of you realize that Dark Arts embraces many, including yourself, and some are not as bad as others.

Spirit Keeping: How?

How? Binding, Vessel Selection, & Spirits

How does Binding work?
Binding is the process of attaching a spirit to a vessel or to a human's spirit. By binding it gives the spirit a home, a chance to be able to share their energy with someone and exchange respect and love. Just like anyone all entities want to feel needed, loved, cared for and that they matter.

There are hundreds of ways to bind a spirit to a vessel or human and most of them involve an invocation. There are only a handful that are publicly shared as most conjurer/practitioner's prefer to keep their binding methods a secret to themselves or amongst their Order, Coven, etc.

Spirits are not harmed during the binding process and are not required to give up anything in return for being bound. Spirits are bound to an object to give the spirit a home and sanctuary of their own. When a spirit is bound to a human's spirit they will usually select an area of the body they like the most and retreat to that part of the body when they feel they need a moment alone.

Binding can take place by using an invocation and binding bag. A binding bag is a satchel that is enchanted with a spell designed specifically for promoting a bind between any spirits that exists to the object in the bag.

You can bind through invocation alone which usually requires the conjurer/practitioner to hold the vessel in their hands while reciting the invocation. Binding can be through rituals using oils, candles, stones and/or statuary associated with the spirit. A spirit can be banished from a vessel releasing them of all ties.

Spirit Keeping: How?

A spirit can be banished from a vessel releasing them of all ties. When a spirit is banished they are no longer tied to the human or vessel any more and are free to be conjured by another conjurer/practitioner or exist without bond. Banishing a spirit is not painful but it is a serious practice that can result in feeling of rejection for both the Keeper and spirit. Before a spirit is banished all other methods of making amends should be explored.

The process by which a conjurer/practitioner binds a spirit is, in part, what dictates the energy with which the spirit will come through to the Keeper and whether or not the spirit could be stolen by a malicious, superior conjurer/practitioner. Though this is a remote chance it does happen between warring collectors which is why publishing or otherwise publicly announcing the name of your spirits is not recommended unless you are 100% positive the conjurer/practitioner who bound the spirit has done so with protection to keep this from happening.

Anyone is capable of learning binding and the first spirits they bind will of course be weak with energy but an entity can be rebound as their powers grow allowing the spirit's capabilities to surface.

Those interested in binding should use meditation techniques to come to a comfortable place before performing the binding action. Being in the right frame of mind is the proper and most effective way to ensure you bind correctly.

How are spirits chosen?

When a conjurer/practitioner performs the act that invites spirits it can be compared to moths to a flame. The energy that is placed out there by the conjurer/practitioner attracts spirits and typically in one act of conjuration no less than three spirits respond within a matter of seconds and want to be pulled. The choice of spirit is left to the discretion of the conjurer/practitioner.

Typically criteria for a spirit to be a good candidate for binding

Spirit Keeping: How?

are their energy, their presence, their demeanor and their abilities. The strongest spirit will always present itself first but depending on the purpose for the binding, and the Keeper the conjurer/practitioner is binding for the first may not always be chosen.

If a conjurer/practitioner is performing a binding specifically for another Keeper the Keeper's needs and personality are always at the forefront of making a spirit choice. Spirits exist in the thousands around all humans at all times and literally hundreds of billions exist within the three realms. It is choosing the proper spirit to bind that is the art and talent of a conjurer/practitioner.

How are vessels chosen?

How vessels are chosen is a question we're often asked. Depending on what is being bound can dictate what kind of vessel is chosen.

For bindings we do often choose vessels of sturdy, unassuming character which is why we love using sterling silver. We would love to have each spirit bound to one of Ash's custom silver pieces but we bind so many spirits that there is no way we could make enough custom pieces fast enough to be able to bind efficiently. So we use jewelry suppliers with whom we can trust their quality. It is important to be able to closely interact with your spirit during the first 30 days and small objects, like jewelry, allow you to be able to be near your entity without anyone in public being the wiser.

When I bind spirits I usually lay out a selection of vessels and allow the spirit to choose what they would like to be bound to. I always lay out the same selection every day: jewelry, gemstones, dolls and statuary and they are left to make the decision.

I find that by giving them a choice they are more energetically bound to the object which works best for everyone all the way around.

Spirit Keeping: How?

As for haunted items that we have come into through estates, trades at paranormal meetings, etc there are times, when dealing with human spirits, they chose the vessel because it is something they loved while alive or were wearing or near when they passed away.

Choosing the right vessel is important when you are binding and it is always suggested you pick a sturdy vessel that can withstand daily use.

If you are learning to bind yourself I suggest having an assortment on hand that contains gemstones, cut or polished. It is important because beginners find binding to gemstones the easiest as the natural, core energy of the Earth helps to pull and connect the spirit.

If you or your spirit decides they want to change their vessel you can use a process we call "Transmuting". We invested a para-technology through which you can move a spirit, spirits, a spell, or spell from one vessel to another; be it all the spirits & spells or a select few from a larger binding. We invented what is called a "Transmute Bag" in order to carry out this process. It moves the spirit or spell from the original vessel to a new vessel without any loss of power, energy, or original structure.

This flexibility is what we always strive to achieve, with this para-technology Keepers have the freedom to make the choices they need to when it comes to their spirits or magic.

Spirit Keeping: Limitations

Limitations, Powers, & Manifestations

I was recently asked about finding an entity that can manifest and exert control over objects, the weather, etc. and I found it an important enough question that it should be covered here.

There are many entities that can manifest in physical form but there are factors involved. First of all, not all have that capability. Secondly, is the likelihood that any entity would manifest to you - do you have second sight? Are you a sensitive person? Have you seen ghosts or manifestations before? Because for something to manifest before you there has to be one of two criteria met - you are either already born with the ability or you have had an entity long enough that it trusts you to do that. Physical manifestations are not to be taken lightly and for those unprepared or not accustomed to such things it may cause a serious health issue. People have been known to suffer small but scary heart attacks, panic attacks, be rendered unconscious, etc. Physical manifestations are usually not controlled by the Keeper but rather a decision made on the behalf of the entity.

The entities most likely to manifest are Dragons and Vampires. Some races of Dragon do present themselves in human form, but again, one of the two criteria has to be met.

As far as the manipulation of tangible objects outside of the realm of Earth law (gravity, physics, biology, etc) that lays largely in the magical ability or potential of the person, not the entity. You could have the most powerful entity that can be contained within this realm and not be able to use it to its fullest potential because of your lack of ability. That is why I tell novices that getting a class 4 or 5 spirit or spelled object, for most people, is something that will last a lifetime because most people do not extend their studies to encompass the root or core magic and strengthen their abilities alongside the abilities of the entity. That's fine

Spirit Keeping: Limitations

because most collectors just want the companionship, the help, the rewards and the natural spiritual growth that comes with keeping a spirit.

When it comes to manipulation of Earthen elements such as the weather (clouds, rain, lightning, thunder, snow, winds, etc), soil (dirt, rocks, sand, stones, minerals), water (any form of liquid), fire (any form of fire), etc. there are many entities whose energies are capable of manipulating and changing the patterns of these elements, but 99% of the time it is within the reason of the Earth and not against the laws of physics, biology, gravity, etc.

Are there entities or people who have these powers? Yes. Are you going to get these powers by owning an entity or spelled piece? Probably not. I would say one in one-hundred million people is born with the ethereal and magical blessings to be able to grow such powers and most of it follows bloodlines. There are some who can educate themselves and find enough experience and wisdom to do one task that defies the laws of the Earth but even then you are still talking one in fifty million people, if that.

I have never known people with these abilities to advertise them, publicly flaunt them or otherwise draw attention to themselves. They don't and for good reason. I know of a coven in Australia and a few people here in the US who have such abilities and they are not going to divulge their secrets and powers themselves. Others may speak of them but you'll never see them or hear from them. They blend into the crowd just like anyone else, because to expose themselves as what they are could cause them serious danger.

Exceptional power lies with many entities but it is the combination of both the natural or learned power of the Keeper and the power of the entity that can yield extraordinary results. If you do not have the power to move boulders or part the seas then you cannot expect a spirit to compensate your lack thereof.

Spirit Keeping: Misconceptions

Misconceptions: Anything Goes in the Spirit World

I absolutely abhor the saying "Anything's possible" when used to describe the paranormal world and/or paranormal collectors. It's absolutely untrue and the ignorance of this statement has led to deaths, injuries, wild misconceptions and problems that cannot even begin to be described in this book. The problems this statement has caused since the beginning of time could fill the Library of Congress easily.

It is a disrespectful saying that completely ignores and shows irreverence to not only the physical realm but the spiritual and astral ones as well. Those who blindly charge full steam ahead with that phrase on their minds have offended the spirits, entities, and gods/goddesses of the physical, astral and spiritual planes, perhaps even unknowingly but nevertheless adherence to that phrase leads you down a bad road.

You cannot say "Well, anything is possible in the paranormal so I'm going to use my Faery's wings and I am going to jump off this building and her wings will make me fly". If you truly believe anything is possible in the world of the paranormal then you should sprout Faery wings when you jump, but you won't will you? You must abide by the laws of the realm we live in.

Every world/realm/plane has rules, counterbalance, and laws that those who inhabit it must abide by.

A Djinn cannot say, "Oh, I'm sick of being a Djinn. I'm just going to become a human now". If anything's possible that could happen right? No, it won't. It never will. Because a Djinn cannot become a human. They do not exist on this plane. They can visit this plane but they do not exist here.

Spirit Keeping: Misconceptions

I have said it before and I will say it until the day I die, the commonly over-used phrase "Anything's possible" is dangerous and the ignorance of knowing the laws and rules by which all realms abide can lead to people showing disrespect to the spirits, entities and god/goddesses of those realms.

Without the structure of each realm abiding by their own rules, restrictions and laws all worlds would be chaos and likely many would have perished long ago.

There are multiple realms and for simplicity's sake we (practitioners/believers) use three: physical, spiritual and astral. Some entities can never cross the borders of their realm. Some can exist in two realms at the same time. Some can travel between two or three realms.

Physical spirits are considered the spirits that lived and existed on Earth at one time.

Spirituals spirits are different entities born to the spiritual plane (e.g. Doppelganger), and any entity that existed on the physical plane has the opportunity to exist on the spiritual plane.
Astral spirits (e.g. Angels, Djinn) were born of and exist within the astral plane. Some astral spirits can enter the physical and spiritual planes as well, like Angels and Djinn.

One of the most common misconceptions in the "Anything's possible" thought-pattern is the crossbreeding of entities... like Djinn-Dragons, Faery-Dragons, etc. and that spirits in spirit form can procreate with one another and have spirit babies.
There is good reason races cannot crossbreed. First of all exactly why would a Djinn mate with a Dragon? That would be like human mating with a lizard! I know its great material for a comic book but in reality or even in the paranormal (not sci-fi) why would a Djinn even mate with a Dragon?

First of all, as I've stated before Dragons and Djinn do not even exist

Spirit Keeping: Misconceptions

of the same energy. Dragons are earth-born creatures and Djinn are astral creatures. If you want to get very basic they don't even relate to each other on any level including speaking the same language. This applies to Fae, Dragons, Djinn, Gargoyles, Angels, Immortals, Leprechauns, and so forth.

Spirits of baby Unicorns, baby Fae, baby "X" all occur because they perished in infancy, not because a spirit procreated. Spirits cannot procreate. Why would they? Why would something that lived and breathed here on Earth go on to die and then experience an existence where they can procreate as spirits? This applies to Dragons, Gargoyles, Vampires, Faeries, etc., as well.

Have Angels, Djinn, and Immortals been known to procreate with humans? Yes. That is different than a spirit procreating with another spirit. Angels, Djinn & Immortals are beings who can manifest on the physical plane but are not from the Earth. You are not talking about a dead human in spirit form procreating with an Angel spirit. I hope you can understand the difference.

As for inter-breeding half-Djinn, half-Dragon, etc., I stand behind my point 100% and outside of eBay I've never seen nor heard of a half-Djinn, half-Dragon entity. I don't understand why a Dragon would mate with a Djinn. In spirit form many do not even resonate on the same plane. However this is not the first time one professional disagreed with another.

Djinn manifested as a Dragon in order to mate with the Dragon and there would be a Dragon baby. But the Dragon baby is half-Dragon, half-Djinn in spirit then? For what purpose though? A Djinn is an astral creature created for many purposes even outside the physical plane. Why would they want to mate with a Dragon? because they form a Liger. But the important point is that they are of the same race, they are both felines. You can't mate a cat and dog. They're both mammals but you won't get a cog or a dat, right?

Spirit Keeping: Misconceptions

The question is not whether or not entities of other planes can procreate... the question is can spirits procreate. Do not confuse the two words (entity & spirit). An entity is still alive; a spirit is the spirit of a perished entity. Why would spirits procreate when they could procreate when they were alive as an entity? There is no purpose for spirits to procreate. They are spirits; they are serving a higher purpose now. And the spiritual plane has plenty of living entities dying & occupying the spiritual plane every day, there's no need to populate an already heavily populated place.

Myths, Lies, and Other Fabrications of Knowledge

It is an unfortunate, but true, fact that the paranormal community can be a tough crowd of cut-throats, frauds, and drama-seekers. It resonates not only through the Spirit Keeping community, but also the psychic, paranormal investigator, and other branches of the paranormal world. This is why you may see on some psychic websites or paranormal investigator websites the plea or promise to keep out of the fray.

The internet makes it very easy for troublemakers to be anonymous and post derogatory comments about their competition posing as buyers or clients. We know, it happened to us over 2007-present. For these reasons & for the reasons that some people like to credit themselves with knowledge they don't possess and "critique" the paranormal community when they truly have no knowledge of what is involved, it is sadly sometimes easy for beginners to find themselves on sites that have less than truthful information.

How can you come by inaccurate information?
*Websites where the person writing the site is not fully acquainted with all the facts.
*Someone who believes themselves more powerful or knowledgeable than they really are.

I can tell you that in doing this for years and the past 3 years with an open forum that you always get people once in awhile who fancy themselves an authority on the subject and intentionally or unintentionally start spreading information about spirits or magic that is completely untrue. You can bet on it happening about once a year. Usually the person befriends other people, seems like a nice person, suddenly they have crazy things to say out of the blue, the people don't know if it's true or not and it leads to stress for everyone involved. As a side note I can tell you that usually people like this have already written in previously to us and have said other off-the-wall things that if known would discredit their reputation with the others they are trying to influence. I've seen this play out enough over the last 3 years. I can write you a play-by-play handbook of how that happens. This has always been a danger in having PM access & email access on our board because people befriend each other and sometimes you have someone who purposefully befriends a number of people with the intent of gaining trust over time & later causing a lot of trouble. You have to weigh the good & bad and try not to limit everyone for the sake of what these people do.

As another side note I should tell you that people who are drama-addicted, crazy, like to cause others turmoil through their own gossip, lies & bile about others are an occupational hazard in the paranormal. In fact, I'd venture to say that the paranormal community as a whole sees more than its share of these kinds of people than perhaps other groups. We have people who are just downright crazy and write in asking if we can burn up the people in the world they don't like, people who write us and pretend to know nothing about magic or spirits and then we find out they are telling others how powerful they are & how they know things. Our community, among others on the net, is about learning. Becoming friends with others in the community be they practitioner or collector is a byproduct of joining communities. As with all things in your life you should just approach personal relationships online with common sense & discretion.

Bound spirits are better than attached spirits...
No, not necessarily. Of course having a binding affords more leeway with being able to provide protection, Bridging, and other positive aspects but in our own home I'd venture to say we have as many bound as unbound living here. Attached spirits come & go and bound spirits chose to be bound & come to you because they want to fulfill a long-term support in your life. There's no greater advantage as far as the

Spirit Keeping: Myths & Lies

spirit's interaction with you, binding only affords you more opportunities for other complementing steps.

Dark Arts = Evil...

Only if you consider yourself evil. Dark Arts means the ability to choose between right or wrong, and humans are Dark Arts beings. We have the freedom to choose to do good or bad the same as Dark Arts spirits. We consider Black Arts entities the ones who operate purely out of evil and they are the ones who have no associations in the Encyclopedia. Dark Arts entities are those who have powers in the white & dark realm of spirits & magic, who you see exacting revenge or vengeance and who can choose to do good or bad in any situation. When a DA is part of your family you do not typically see them acting out against those in their own family circle because they are also very loyal beings.

Spirits travel in families...

Typically, no. This is an assumption where it depends on what entity you are talking about. There will always be exceptions but 99% of the time they do not.

You can forcibly bind spirits...

Yes, but in order to do so you better be extremely powerful and you WILL pay for it with your own energy, spirit & karma. You typically only see this in black magic practitioners doing so against other Black Arts spirits to force them to do their bidding because Black Arts spirits as a rule will not voluntarily help you. However, it should also be noted that in this case the word "spirit" is inaccurate because most of the time the Black Arts "spirits" bound against their will are living entities who reside on another plane such as the astral or spiritual. BA practitioners always pay in the end. You don't usually see their run last longer than a few months or a year before something breaks them down if they are going with the forcible approach. BA entities have powers beyond any scope of a human and typically a BA practitioner will allow themselves to become possessed by a strong BA spirit in order to continue BA work. The number of these kinds of practitioners are few and far between.

Spirit Keeping: Myths & Lies

You can kidnap spirits...
No. They are not vulnerable, unknowing beings floating around waiting to be taken advantage of. They require respect and often humility to bring them through conjuration and they choose whether or not to come to you. Your reciting a conjuration opens the gate for any spirit(s) who want to come forward to do so to you specifically. Think about the words being a key turning the lock on a door and when you're done the door opens to the spiritual or astral realms. You cannot do a spiritual drive-by and scoop up unsuspecting spirits... I apologize if you think I am making light of it, but this is one of the most ludicrous things I've heard to date. Spirits demand respect, rightly so, and you have to give respect to get it in the Spiritual world.

You can torture or beat spirits...
The context of that expression denies itself. A spirit is a spirit therefore you cannot physically injure it. Are there nasty people in the world who have spirits to drag them down with themselves and be verbally abusive? Sure. Nasty people are everywhere but you have to remember we're talking about spirits. The spirit has the opportunity to move itself from the physical to spiritual plane at their own will and that is something you cannot take away from them no matter who you are. If they are not liking a situation they are in they are going to move to the spiritual and/or astral plane. As I've said before, humans are human. People have to get off the mindset that humans are superior beings, we are not, and we are graced by the presence of spirits, not the other way around. Spirits are far more advanced than we. If a spirit is permanently bound to a vessel and not attached then they will likely go into the spiritual or astral realm to reside and not be with the vessel on the physical plane.

Spirits procreate...
Spirits do not have babies, they are spirits. They may have had babies when they were alive and they may go through those motions or relive those memories with you. They may bring those other spirits into your life once they are settled but this is

Spirit Keeping: Myths & Lies

not the norm as stated above about spirit families. They do not usually bring others into an existing situation 99% of the time.

As said before there are exceptions to this. Keepers with unique energy may promote that kind of behavior, but the majority of the time you aren't going to have a spirit bring other spirits to you without your consent or knowledge. Respect & trust is a two-way street and you will see that spirits abide by respect & trust.

Binding to Spirit = Soul binding
No. We don't do it, and we don't advocate for anyone who is thinking about it. Binding to spirit means binding to your essence, the field of energy that comprises your unique spirit, which some believe is split into pieces & reincarnated, while your soul moves on to whatever you believe is your version of Heaven. So if someone tells you Binding to Spirit means soul binding you can tell them they are ignorant of the facts.

You can kill a spirit...
No, that would be what is known as an oxymoron. A spirit is a spirit because it was once a living entity and now it is not, so it is in spirit form. An entity is a being that is still alive on any plane or in any dimension. When that living entity expires most come into spirit form. Immortals, like Aphrodite & Zeus for example, are not spirits because they are Immortal so they are living beings that continue to live without expiry. You can banish a spirit back where it came from but you cannot kill it. Do not work with practitioners who believe they are more powerful than spirits or magic because their lack of respect could bring you serious problems. You must exercise respect & humility when working with the paranormal.

Spirits are all-powerful...
Absolutely not. Dying and moving into spirit form does not mean you've just won some kind of universal power contest. If the spirit did not have the power while in living form it will not have it in death. Yes, spirits do

Spirit Keeping: Myths & Lies

come into some abilities like moving between the physical & spiritual planes but if they were not magically-inclined in life they are not going to know or be able to practice magic just because they came into spirit form. That goes for any ability or power. A Harpy, for instance, is not going to suddenly become and emblem of Good Luck & Attracting Positive Light because they are now a spirit, just as a Leprechaun is not going to become a powerful sorcerer in spirit form. Spirits do not come into cosmic powers they did not have in life just because they died.

All Conjurations or Summoning practices are evil...
A conjuration or a summon is to call upon an entity or a spirit. To summon something doesn't have to be complicated; when they call out for help to God or they call out for the angels to help them, they are summoning those entities for help. You can summon or call many kinds of entities from pure white to grey to pure black. To bind is the process of taking the next step after conjuring or summoning and the entity must give consent in order to be bound.

Conjuring, Summoning & Channeling: 3 very different things...
Conjuring is the process of using an invocation or ritual to bring an entity or spirit through to you. Mastery of this takes time & often years. Those who are not experienced or masters should not write conjurations as choice of word & conjuration formation is essential to conjuring the right entity. Conjurations given away or sold by masters can be used by the novice & intermediate for trusted results. The invocation for conjuration & instructions provided (if any) should be followed to the letter.

Summoning is the process of calling an entity or spirit. It is not always 100% accurate when used simply as a call to an Angel, for example. The more specific you are in summoning the better off you are. It has little or no structure provided and therefore calling out for assistance could result in any entity willing to respond to do so. Summoning does not require invocations or rituals and can be done through verbal

Spirit Keeping: Myths & Lies

expression, use of a vessel, or telepathy.

Channeling is the process of connecting yourself to another entity or place; it is temporary and does not require immediate presence in one location like Conjuring or Summoning. Neither you nor the target has to leave your current location to channel.

For instance, you can channel the spirit of a lost relative on the spiritual plane. You are extending your energy to them on their realm and creating a connection. You can channel a location in the astral realm, you can astral travel and channel a time, place, or person. Channeling is an explorative method used to help you in discovery & growth of your energy & abilities. Channeling often requires an invocation or a method of visualization. Sometimes the channeling invocation can be bound to an object which is then activated by the user in some manner.

Can someone steal your spirits, or can a practitioner call back a spirit they bound?
In a nutshell, no. We can only truly speak for Creepy Hollows when we say spirits are never called back unless the Keeper requests them to be. When we conjure & bind a spirit we do so without any bonding, without any personal interaction, and provide only the basic details as given during conjuration for the next Keeper to identify with. We do this because we have no interest in becoming personally invested with a spirit we plan to home. Yes, it leads to non-lengthy descriptions, but we conjure for the purpose of homing and not the purpose of bonding with them.

Can someone steal your spirits from their vessels? No. Why?
#1 to unbind you must know the process in which it was bound
#2 you cannot forcibly bind spirits
#3 we cannot transmute any spirits whose vessels are lost without their permission because as #2 states, you cannot force a spirit to be bound.

For example, I can't take one of Gwen's Werewolves from a vessel nor

Spirit Keeping: Myths & Lies

can she take a Vampire binding we've done from a vessel. Not only that, but conjurer/practitioners have no reason to try; they are capable of conjuring spirits so why would they want to do that when they can conjure what they want?

Binding isn't a simple thing you can do without either training or without a tool already prepared with the necessary enchantments for you to activate. Unbinding requires you to know how it was bound in order to deconstruct the binding and reverse the process. Not to mention any conjurer/practitioner worth their weight in gold will place certain enchantments on their bindings to safeguard the spirits & spells from anyone trying to be bothersome. We have talked about that in another section.

Spirits can leave you whenever they want forever or temporarily?
If you have a spirit that has been bound then no, they can't leave the binding forever. Spirits do move between the different realms (which realms depends on the type of spirit) which may account for their temporary absence sometimes.

A spirit cannot, however, decide to remove themselves from you indefinitely. If someone tells you this I would strongly question their motives for telling you that. Are they trying to sell you a product or service to bring the spirit back? Are they offering to be a medium between you & the spirit and convince them to come back, or any other such nonsense? I cannot say it enough that spirits are not emotional beings that are going to have a hissy fit and stomp away. Rather, they are evolved beings that are fully capable of making sound decisions based on the fact they can see beyond what we mortals can and in coming to you in the first place they had a reason for being with you! A bound spirit has the freedom to move between this realm & their own, but they can't unbind themselves from a vessel.

Check for the latest updates to the Myths & Lies information in our Forum http://www.creepyhollows.com

Spirit Keeping: Different Realms

The Different Realms

When we speak about different entities from different realms we are speaking about three realms in particular - Earthen, Spiritual & Astral.

Earthen :: The planet Earth. This is the realm our physical bodies reside within. There are literally hundreds of thousands of races of entities who have been born and become extinct on this realm. Thousands of mystical entities exist within this realm alone and are capable of peacefully coexisting with humans. This realm is a grounding area useful for humans to make a connection with Mother Nature and the Earth's core powers.

It is a birthplace of mystical knowledge, a gateway to both the Spiritual and Astral realms and represents a median point for human existence. Its fragility is also its strength, lending an ever changing atmosphere for the entities residing within it to grow and adapt. It possesses alone extraordinary powers giving those who seek them a vast influence and giving everyone on the planet a taste of its capabilities through its natural disasters. Just as the other realms this one holds an unimaginable trove of secrets from its ocean floor, under and above water caves, soil, sand, lava... and swirling through its atmosphere the spiritual stains left by billions of entities since the beginning of time. With each century bringing a more dense air clouded with the spiritual energy of those billions passed.

Spiritual :: The realm that serves as an originating point and a gateway to other realms. All entities who exist on Earth will pass through the Spiritual realm at death on their way to the afterlife. There are many entities who find life starts within the spiritual realm; most of the races are guardian races who serve both Astral entities and Earthen entities.

The Spiritual realm is buzzing with energy and can be both a torrential source of power and a tender comfort. It is the gateway for humans to make connections with humans who

Spirit Keeping: Different Realms

have passed. Those who wish to exert medium powers will find the Spiritual realm is their platform for communication.

It exists within and around humans allowing any who are open to making a connection a swift retrieval of spiritual energy. Humans are capable of existing within the Earthen and Spiritual realm simultaneously when in the proper state of mind. On a basic level humans who practice religion find themselves often within both realms such as in times of prayer, meditation, traditional ceremonies, etc. On a more intense level those who practice Spiritualism can walk both planes at the same time maximizing their powers of greater influence with entities and spirits in both realms.

Astral :: The realm of the heavens. All Immortal entities exist within this realm as well as Djinn and Angels amongst others. It is a realm of tremendous mystery as it holds the most power and possibilities. The Astral realm is a beacon of pure light and a strong source of compelling energies.

The energies of the Astral realm are ethereal and can leave a lasting impression on a human when they first experience what the realm has to offer. Some have walked through one of the astral portals that exist on Earth's realm and have described it as being wrapped by a warm blanket, the pure feeling of happiness, and a tingling sensation at the base of the neck, spine or throat. Astral portals are a natural occurrence on Earth and though the chance a human will accidentally walk into one is one in a million those who are lucky enough never forget. The portals do not transport humans, but it is rather a gathering of energy that comes and goes. Astral entities can walk all three realms at the same time at their discretion. They are gifted with this ability and therefore can exact great influence over entities of all the realms. They are capable of providing life-altering magic to humans and spirits. The Astral realm is the pinnacle of mystic connection and power.

Spirit Keeping: Spiritualism

What is Spiritualism?

There are many branches of Spiritualism practiced worldwide. Our branch and what our site is dedicated to is the practice of Spiritualism where the person participating collects the spirits of entities for the purpose of giving them a renewed life and mutual exchange of energy.

Spiritualism is the belief in and practice of binding the spirits of the three main planes - earthen, spiritual and astral, to vessels or self for the purpose of collecting, companionship and exchange of energy and power. Vessels can be of monetary value or sentimental value ranging from diamonds and gold to quilts and pottery shards. It is not the vessel but what is bound to it that dictates the value to Spiritualist collectors.

Examples of spirits that may be bound are Humans, Dragons, Immortals, Fae, Creatures, Angels, Djinn, Vampires, Gargoyles and the like.

Spiritualism often begins as a hobby and becomes a way of life. Because it is encompassing of all religious subscriptions Spiritualism is a widely accepted and practiced form of spiritual guidance and journey. Our current family of collectors includes the following faiths: Agnostic, Atheist, Buddhist, Christian, Gnostic, Jewish, Muslim, Polytheistic, Wiccan and other major religions. It transcends religious boundaries because Spiritualism unites its collectors through the commonality of experiencing life beyond that which is considered "normal". We as a group believe there is more to life than meets the eyes and are ready to partake in the adventure of learning what secrets the Earth and other realms hold.

The collection and care of spirits is not a novelty, it is a responsibility. Keepers often find that their spirits become a member of their family and can even become close and contact other members of the Keeper's family if they reach out and welcome the spirit too. Once a spirit is bound to a vessel they

Spirit Keeping: Spiritualism

are bound for eternity unless banished through a banishing ritual. If a spirit is bound directly to a human the spirit remains bound unless banished or until the human passes away. There is a school of thought, however, that the spirit can accompany the human into the afterlife.

There are different ways in which a Spiritualist can live their life. It can be any combination of the following examples and often is. Spiritualists usually find themselves working their way towards making it a lifestyle as opposed to a hobby.

Collectors :: Those who collect the spirits conjured by master Spiritualists.
Investigators :: Those who investigate the presence of spirits in edifices and nature. They attempt to identify the purpose of the spirit's presence and the history behind their presence in the location.
Researchers :: Those who research the chronology of spirits discovered, attempting to locate the origin, identify the behavior, learn the life span, powers and community associated with the spirit.
Practitioners :: Those who are skilled in the art of conjuration and binding of the spirits to vessels or humans as an attempt to preserve their existence.

For those who are truly immersed it is an entirely new way of experiencing the Earth and life on it. It's a faith with the ability to realize that you do not belong to the earth, that the earth belongs to you. It is a gift to be enjoyed and it is much more mystical and wonderful than trips to the store or a 9 to 5 job. It's a playground of history, legend and every entity from a million years ago to right this moment linked together by common energy.

Your entire view of life awakens to the true beauties that you were not able to appreciate before. Life as a Spiritualist opens you to a wealth of adventures, wisdom, experiences, and joys that can truly make all the difference in your life.

Spirit Keeping: A Guide for Spirit Keepers

Being a Spiritualist opens you to experience the spirits you interact with. This includes the ability to see, hear and interact with physical manifestations such as ghosts and Fae. The ability to communicate with spiritual entities through visions, psychic intuition, intrinsic knowledge, meditation communication, audible contact, and more. For Keepers the interaction between themselves and the spirit is paramount to a good relationship.

Spiritualism vs. Religion

Spiritualism should never be thought of as a religion on its own; rather it is a complementing belief to any existing religion or lifestyle. The belief, practice and collection of spirits should be considered a benefit and honor that accompanies you through your religious journey and the lifestyle of a Spiritualist as an enhancement to your religious beliefs. This thought process allows humans of all religions and lifestyles to be able to share a common bond and grants the opportunity for a second family atmosphere where each can learn from another. This affords not only the spirits but the Keepers to be enlightened and gain valuable wisdom.

No matter your religious subscription, you will find that Spiritualism works within the boundaries of your beliefs. All religions believe in paranormal events, the abilities of a said stronger force of power, guidance, creation, etc. There is a "god" to everyone and even if it is not the same god there are so many similarities that religious practitioners across the world can complement their lives with the practice of Spiritualism. You do not have to abandon your beliefs to collect. Rather, you will find that collecting and spending so much time creating the mystic connection between yourself and the spiritual world brings you closer to your religious doctrine and your god.

Do not shy away from bringing your spirits into your religious practices. Welcome them to partake of your daily, weekly, or monthly rituals, bring them to your church, synagogue or temple, recite prayers with them. Don't feel you have to keep them separate because it isn't so. By exercising your religious beliefs with them you will find a closer connection all the way around.

With Spiritualism as a community of collectors, the difference of opinions, lifestyles and religions makes for a very strong community. For many this becomes a community they consider not only friends but family. You will find that more often than not

Spirit Keeping: Spiritualism vs. Religion

your fellow community members are open-minded, wanting to learn about you and your beliefs and are not quick to judge or condemn.

When you collect the paranormal you will find the most diverse company around you. There are collectors from every walk of life, every religion, every background who walk beside you!

To examine the most widely expressed religions; Catholicism & Christianity, Catholics are by far the most mystical and paranormal Christians. They believe in the most amazing miracles, they believe ordinary objects have paranormal powers, and their clergy holds paranormal powers. They collect and honor relics of paranormal powers. They are incredibly superstitious, have rituals and blessings, harbor centuries old mystical secrets and a large number of other key factors.

Catholics are not alone, as many Christians believe in many different belief systems ranging from the powers of God, the powers of Jesus and the power of many of God's chosen people.

While some Christian religions are very prudent in belief others are wide open to possibilities. As we are Gnostics we believe in the mystic connection between God and His children as many of the disciples such as Thomas did. We recommend the reading of the Gospel of Thomas as it is highly intellectual and widely appreciated for its mystical references. It is our belief that we all worship the same God, we just all know Him by different names & manifestations. For this reason we do not admonish or take lightly anyone's beliefs.

We believe it is absolutely possible God created Unicorns, Pegasus, Dragons, Djinn, Faeries, Phoenix, and any other mystical creature. We do not rule out anything as it is not for us to judge what God is capable of... who are we to say how powerful He is? I certainly am not going to take it upon myself to judge what a supreme being is capable of doing when I am not as wise, powerful and capable as He. For those of you

Spirit Keeping: Spiritualism vs. Religion

who know the ancient texts, creatures such as the Unicorn were in the Bible before the churches made their own translations leaving out many mystic details. There are many Discovery Channel specials on these topics and they are each worth seeing.

There are other religions as well who take a very mystic view of the world and we celebrate them all! Agnosticism... Animism... Atheism... Buddhism... Candomble... Catholicism... Christian... Egyptian... Gnosticism... Hinduism... Islam...Judaism... Jainism... Paganism... Shinto... Taoism... Unitarianism... Wicca... Zoroastrianism... and all others!

There is something to be learned from everyone and everything around you. A closed mind will wither and never have the chance to grow. Don't be a judge, be a student and watch how your life blossoms and grows. Learn about the world, the people, the religions, the beliefs, and the creatures around you... celebrate life!

Yes, there is an ultimate being in charge, an ultimate center of creation. Recorded history is a pea-sized amount of what can actually be derived as the truth. As you know, only the select few in times of Moses, Jesus, Buddha, and so on were educated enough to record history and with any human endeavor the odds that someone recorded history without imposing their own prejudice is not likely. We already know that the early church omitted texts from the Bible because they did not agree with what was written. That tells you that it is likely all other religious texts are prone to sway to what the originator of the document wants you to think.

It is not at all impossible that we are all worshipping the same central being... that Buddha, Jesus, Allah and others are the same being just recorded differently in history.

If you believe that the tribes were scattered across the Earth then you know that some settled the Middle East, others Egypt, others Italy, and

Spirit Keeping: Spiritualism vs. Religion

others Greece. If you look at the central starting point of the main religions recognized in these countries you will find an extremely similar story that commonly links each. Each religion grew into its own with time as each ruler, priest, noble and worshipper experienced their own revelations, enlightenment and interactions. So are each wrong? No, because an entity that is capable of creating universes, heavens, realms, etc is far more intelligent than we are capable of comprehending.

In Romans 1:18 of the protestant Bible it says: "18The wrath of God is being revealed from heaven against all the godlessness and wickedness of men who suppress the truth by their wickedness, 19since what may be known about God is plain to them, because God has made it plain to them. 20For since the creation of the world God's invisible qualities-his eternal power and divine nature-have been clearly seen, being understood from what has been made, so that men are without excuse."

So if you are to believe that God makes Himself known to everyone, even a small tribe in the abyss of the African jungle do you think that they would call him "God" or would they call him something of their native tongue that would sound like "Obigabi" to us? So in the limited judgment of those who traveled and explored the African jungle they would say the tribe's people were pagans because they worshipped "Obigabi", but in fact they worship the same God as everyone else.

Every person has their unique interactions with God, however you perceive God, and if you were completely devoid of your prejudiced knowledge and it was left to you to record history how would you record what has happened to you? What names would you use? What situations and interactions would you use to describe your life, your revelations, your visions?

Believers know, in limited mortal intelligence, that God is well aware of what happens on Earth and probably saw all of it play out before He even created the first grain of sand so it is prudent not to be short-sighted enough to think that we are all worshipping different gods. We could be worshipping the same God but in different ways. As the population grew and moved at the start of civilization different people recorded their interactions with the divine in different ways. They, naturally, had their own names for what they interacted with.

All Immortals from all civilizations are ethereal beings. They are of the same origin as Djinn and Angels. Since every religion has their own "versions" of Immortals it would stand to reason that they are all connected one to another by the same source of creation.

Once you can see that in ancient history we are limited to literally a handful out of thousands who were educated enough to record history in writing, you understand that there are millions of lives who had experiences that were never recorded because of the lack of education. Instead we are left with the limited view and tiny window left by the handful of humans who were capable of writing.

Conclusion

Thank you for taking the time to read these materials. We have been doing this a very long time and there is no doubt that newcomers have lots of questions. We hope this covers the initial aspects of what Spirit Keeping is and how to be a good Spirit Keeper. We have maintained being leaders in the field of the paranormal by living it every day and helping those who need information, education, or advice along the way.

For additional resources and if you have additional questions, we are going to refer you to our website, www.creepyhollows.com

There you can join the forum with hundreds of members who can also provide you with advice & thoughts. You can read our ever-growing Encyclopedia for articles, spirit Associations, How-To's, and other tidbits of knowledge. Enjoy the rest of the site, which offers an extensive Online Store, and a Marketplace for other practitioners & collectors to offer listings of services & goods.

We also own the world's largest collection of paranormal artifacts (non-spirited, and non-spelled). You can see more information regarding that in our Paranormal Collector magazine (available for purchase in our Online Store), and by visiting our site www.paranormalcollector.com

Dictionary of commonly used terms & terms coined by Creepy Hollows

Attaching/Attachment : describing the state of a spirit it typically describes unbounds who have attached themselves to a physical object. The spirit can choose to unattach themselves at any time. Sometimes people are aware of attached spirits, sometimes not.

Binding/Bound : describing the state of a spirit it means a practitioner has created a binding to a physical object or to someone's spirit where the spirit has an immediate method of contact & interaction with the human. They do not live within the object, are capable of returning to their own realm(s), and merely gives a "home base" for the spirit & Keeper to communicate. It is a permanent action.

Black Arts (BA) : a ranking of black means it will typically choose evil, wrongdoing or to act out against its Keeper or anyone else around them. A ranking of black means the magic, spell or enchantment is of black or dark origin.

Channeling : the process of connecting yourself to another entity or place. It is temporary and does not require immediate presence in one location like Conjuring or Summoning. Neither you nor the target has to leave your current location to channel. For instance, you can channel the spirit of a lost relative on the spiritual plane. You are extending your energy to them on their realm and creating a connection. You can channel a location in the astral realm, you can astral travel and channel a time, place, or person. Channeling is an explorative method used to help you in discovery & growth of your energy & abilities. Channeling often requires an invocation or a method of visualization. Sometimes the channeling invocation can be bound to an object which is then activated by the user in some manner.

Charging*: any method, through container or spell, that refreshes & rejuvenates a spirit to peak energy.

Cloak/Cloud/Shadow Spirit*: all techniques that can be utilized by a practitioner to fool an outsider who does not own the spirited or spelled vessel from seeing what is truly bound to the vessel. This can be something like the Dead Spell where a vessel is rendered "empty"

Spirit Keeping: Dictionary

to outsiders. Cloaks typically hide a binding completely, Clouds usually confuse someone into not really knowing what they seeing, Shadow Spirits are manifestations of a fake spirit so the outsider can't see what is really there. Shadow Spirits can also be scary in appearance to frighten the nosy outsider.

Code Words* : powerful word(s) used to immediately provoke the energies or powers of a spirit or spell. They can be used on their own or incorporated into spells, rituals, ceremonies, meditation, etc.

Conjuring : process of using an invocation or ritual to bring an entity or spirit through to you. Mastery of this takes time & often years. Those who are not experienced or masters should not write conjurations as choice of word & conjuration formation is essential to conjuring the right entity. Conjurations given away or sold by masters can be used by the novice & intermediate for trusted results and the invocation for conjuration & instructions provided (if any) should be followed to the letter.

Dark Arts (DA) or Grey Arts (GA) : a ranking of grey/dark means that is like a human; capable of good and bad. They will likely choose good but can experience ups & downs in mood & energy just like us.
A ranking of grey/dark means the magic, spell or enchantment is a balance of white & dark magic and is a neutral force, OR the energy is macabre, dark, rooted in dark origin.

Draw* : describes a support tool used to "draw" an experience or interaction from a spirit or spell. For example: a candle, stone, incense, oil, code words, etc.

Energy signature* : each person's unique energy profile that is used by practitioners & spirits to identify one individual from another.

Entity : being that is currently living its lifetime and will eventually pass into spirit form, or is an Immortal and cannot pass into spirit form.
This word is, however, often used to describe any paranormal being and should be evaluated in its context to derive the meaning.

Immortal : a being that is incapable of dying through any means. Gods & goddesses are the primary example of Immortals.

Invoke/Invocation : a string of words in short or long form used to invoke an action, energy, or spirit. These words can be read out loud

Spirit Keeping: Dictionary

or said through telepathy

Layering*: using multiple layers of spells to create a complex network of spell-blends, or multiple layers of protection & safeguards to protect a spirit. You can also use layers to provide a spirit multiple layers of amenities at time of binding; including Charging energy, offerings of complementary spells to their power, and so forth.

Neutral Arts/Energy : energy that exists of a paranormal level but does not have any intention or motivation. It is neither white or dark. It can be channeled & used as white or dark in efforts, or used on its own as simply a paranormal energy source.

Paranormal Collector : someone who collects items that emit a paranormal energy through natural occurrence, magic, or spirit.

Portal : an opening between realms which can be used to transport one's self from one realm to another in physical, spiritual, or astral form. Portals occur naturally or can be opened & closed through invocation (portal keys).

Portal Keys : a string of words used to create an opening between two realms; known as a portal.

Spirit : being that lived a life and died on the physical, spiritual, or astral realm. The spirit is the essence of the once living being and retains their core "self". It is not to be confused with the soul, which is the divine aspect of each living being that moves onto their respective "heaven". There are tens of thousands of different entities known to exist that pass into spirit form, and billions of spirits from the tens of thousands of races that exist on the physical, spiritual, and astral realms. Many spirits are open to sharing their existence with humans as a shared life exchanging the benefits each offers to the other.

Spirit Keeper* : someone who collects bindings of spirits of various nature to complement their life in multiple aspects.

Spirit Stone* : gemstones specially prepared to be a home to a spirit of any origin.

Summoning : process of calling an entity or spirit. It is not always 100% accurate when used simply as a call to an Angel. The more specific you are in summoning, the better off you are. It has little or no

Spirit Keeping: Dictionary

structure provided and therefore calling out for assistance could result in any entity willing to respond to do so. Summoning does not require invocations or rituals and can be done through verbal expression, use of a vessel, or telepathy.

Transmute* : the process of moving spirits and/or spells, in whole or part, from one vessel to another.

Unbounds : spirits that roam without any obligation to a specific person or place.

Vessel : what is used to bind a spirit or spell for keeping by a human. A vessel can be a tangible object like jewelry or gemstones, or can be the person's spirit.

White Arts (WA) : A ranking of white means the spirit is good, positive, has an uplifting & kind energy associated with it. A ranking of white means the magic, spell or enchantment is of a positive, white light origin.

* Indicates a word or term coined by Creepy Hollows to describe an aspect of Paranormal Collecting.

Spirit Keeping: Section for Your Notes

Spirit Keeping: Section for Your Notes

Spirit Keeping: Section for Your Notes

Spirit Keeping: Section for Your Notes

Spirit Keeping: Section for Your Notes

Spirit Keeping: Section for Your Notes